A
Betty Crocker
PICTURE COOKBOOK
Meatless Main Dishes

D0696641

GOLDEN PRESS/NEW YORK
Western Publishing Company, Inc.
Racine, Wisconsin

Copyright © 1982, 1975 by General Mills, Inc., Minneapolis, Minn.
All rights reserved. Produced in the U.S.A.

Library of Congress Catalog Card Number: 81-83378
ISBN 0-307-09665-3

Golden® and Golden Press® are trademarks of
Western Publishing Company, Inc.

CONTENTS

Fill each trout with about ½ cup of the stuffing; arrange trout in greased baking dish.

Lightly butter 4 strips (6x3 inches each) of foil, then wrap tails of trout and bake.

Stuffed Baked Trout

- 2 medium green peppers, chopped (about 2 cups)
- 1 can (4 ounces) sliced mushrooms, drained
- ½ cup butter or margarine
- 20 cherry tomatoes, cut in half
- 2 cups herb-seasoned croutons
- ¼ cup lemon juice
- 2 teaspoons salt
- ¼ teaspoon pepper
- ¼ teaspoon dried marjoram leaves
  Salt
- 4 trout (10 to 12 ounces each)
  Lemon slices
  Cucumber slices
  Cherry tomatoes

Heat oven to 350°. Cook and stir green pepper and mushrooms in butter until green pepper is tender, about 5 minutes. Remove from heat. Stir in cherry tomato halves, croutons, lemon juice, 2 teaspoons salt, the pepper and marjoram.

Lightly salt the cavity of each trout; fill with ½ cup of the stuffing. Place remaining stuffing in greased 1-quart casserole. Arrange trout in greased baking dish, 13½x8¾x1¾ inches. Wrap tails in buttered aluminum foil. Bake stuffing and trout until trout flakes easily with fork, 30 to 35 minutes.

Remove foil from tails. Garnish with lemon slices, cucumber slices and cherry tomatoes.   4 SERVINGS.

Cut each frozen block of fish into 3 equal parts. Arrange in ungreased baking dish.

Spread with sauce, half of the cheese, the zucchini, garlic salt and remaining cheese.

Parmesan Fish Italiano

2 packages (1 pound each) frozen fish fillets
1 teaspoon salt
  Tomato-Chili Sauce (below)
¼ cup grated Parmesan cheese
1 pound zucchini, cut crosswise into ¼-inch
  slices
½ teaspoon garlic salt

Heat oven to 475°. Cut each frozen block of fish into 3 parts. (Let stand at room temperature 10 minutes before cutting.) Arrange fish in ungreased baking dish, 11¾x7½x1¾ inches. Sprinkle fish with salt. Prepare Tomato-Chili Sauce; spread 1 tablespoon over each part fish. Sprinkle with 2 tablespoons of the cheese. Arrange zucchini slices on fish; sprinkle with garlic salt and remaining cheese. Bake uncovered until fish flakes easily with fork, about 1 hour. Serve with remaining Tomato-Chili Sauce.   6 SERVINGS.

TOMATO-CHILI SAUCE

1 bottle (12 ounces) chili sauce
1 tablespoon prepared horseradish
1 tablespoon lemon juice
½ teaspoon Worcestershire sauce
¼ teaspoon salt

Heat all ingredients to boiling, stirring occasionally.

Baked Codfish

2 medium onions, thinly sliced
2 tablespoons butter or margarine
2 tablespoons olive or vegetable oil
2 pounds codfish, cut into 1-inch pieces
  Broth Béchamel (right)
2 pounds small new potatoes, cooked,
  peeled and cut into ¼-inch slices
6 hard-cooked eggs, sliced
¼ cup snipped parsley
½ teaspoon salt
½ teaspoon lemon pepper

Cook and stir onion slices in butter and oil in 12-inch
skillet until tender. Stir in codfish. Cook uncovered over
low heat 30 minutes. Prepare Broth Béchamel.

Heat oven to 350°. Layer half each of the codfish and onions, potatoes, eggs and Broth Béchamel in ungreased baking dish, 11¾x7½x1¾ inches. Sprinkle with half each of
the parsley, salt and lemon pepper. Repeat. Bake uncovered until light brown and bubbly, about 45 minutes.
8 TO 10 SERVINGS.

Stir the codfish into sautéed
onions; cook 30 minutes.

Layer ingredients; add parsley,
salt, lemon pepper. Repeat.

BROTH BECHAMEL

¼ cup butter or margarine
¼ cup all-purpose flour
½ teaspoon salt
⅛ teaspoon pepper
1 cup chicken broth
1 cup milk
2 tablespoons catsup

Cook and stir butter, flour, salt and pepper over low heat until mixture is smooth and bubbly, about 2 minutes. Remove from heat. Stir in broth, milk and catsup. Heat to boiling, stirring constantly. Boil and stir 1 minute.

Add croutons, corn, tomato, cheese, onion to egg mixture.

Arrange halibut on croutons; top with remaining croutons.

Crouton-Halibut Bake

2 pounds frozen skinless halibut fillets, thawed*
1 teaspoon salt
½ cup mayonnaise or salad dressing
2 tablespoons lemon juice
1 egg, beaten
2 cups seasoned croutons
1 cup drained whole kernel corn with sweet peppers
1 medium tomato, chopped (about ¾ cup)
¼ cup grated American cheese food
2 tablespoons instant minced onion
Lemon slices

Heat oven to 350°. Sprinkle halibut with salt. Mix mayonnaise, lemon juice and egg in medium bowl. Stir in croutons, corn, tomato, cheese and onion. Spread 2 cups of the crouton mixture in greased baking dish, 11¾x7½x1¾ inches. Arrange halibut on top; spread with remaining crouton mixture.

Bake uncovered until halibut flakes easily with fork, 45 to 50 minutes. Garnish with lemon slices.   6 SERVINGS.

*Cod, pollack, flounder or sole can be substituted for the halibut.

Two-Fish Slaw

1 pound skinless flounder, torsk or cod fillets
2 tablespoons lemon juice
½ small head cabbage, shredded (about 3 cups)
1 large stalk celery, cut into thin diagonal slices (about 1 cup)
1 can (4½ ounces) tiny shrimp, rinsed and drained
¾ cup mayonnaise or salad dressing
3 tablespoons lemon juice
¾ to 1 teaspoon salt
½ teaspoon dried basil leaves
Salad greens
Cherry tomatoes
Parsley sprigs

Heat water (1½ inches) to boiling in 10-inch skillet or Dutch oven. Add flounder fillets and 2 tablespoons lemon juice; reduce heat. Simmer uncovered until flounder flakes easily with fork, 8 to 10 minutes. (Cooking time varies according to thickness of flounder.) Remove flounder from skillet; drain and flake.

Place flounder, cabbage, celery and shrimp in large bowl. Mix mayonnaise, 3 tablespoons lemon juice, the salt and basil; pour on flounder mixture and toss. Cover and refrigerate about 2 hours.

Spoon slaw onto salad greens. Core tomatoes; insert a parsley sprig in each tomato. Garnish salad with tomatoes. 6 SERVINGS.

Simmer flounder until it flakes easily with a fork. Drain and flake the flounder.

Place flounder, shredded cabbage, celery and shrimp in a large bowl.

Mix the mayonnaise, 3 tablespoons lemon juice, the salt and the dried basil leaves.

Pour the dressing on the flounder mixture and toss. Cover and refrigerate 2 hours.

To make fancy garnishes for fish, use carrots, carrot tops, eggs, dill pickles topped with onions and mild sweet peppers.

Or try whole or grated radishes, lemon slices or peel, cherry tomatoes on lettuce or cucumber slices with parsley sprigs.

Dilled Torsk

- **2 pounds frozen skinless torsk fillets, thawed**
- **3 tablespoons butter or margarine, softened**
- **2 tablespoons lemon juice**
- **1 teaspoon dried dill weed**
- **½ teaspoon salt**
- **¼ teaspoon paprika**
  Tomato wedges

Heat oven to 375°. Place torsk fillets in ungreased baking dish, 11¾x7½x1¾ inches. Brush both sides of torsk with butter. Sprinkle both sides with lemon juice, dill and salt. Sprinkle tops with paprika. Bake uncovered until torsk flakes easily with fork, 30 to 35 minutes. Garnish with tomato wedges and parsley.   4 OR 5 SERVINGS.

Barbecued Fish

1 pound frozen skinless fish fillets, thawed
¼ cup catsup
3 tablespoons lemon juice
1 tablespoon Worcestershire sauce
2 teaspoons sugar
2 teaspoons instant minced onion
¼ teaspoon salt
   Dash of red pepper sauce
   Lemon wedges

Place fish fillets in ungreased baking pan, 13x9x2 inches. Mix catsup, lemon juice, Worcestershire sauce, sugar, onion, salt and pepper sauce. Pour on fish; turn until both sides are coated. Cover and refrigerate 30 minutes.

Heat oven to 400°. Bake uncovered until fish flakes easily with fork, 15 to 20 minutes. Garnish with lemon wedges. Serve with pan juices.　　3 OR 4 SERVINGS.

Fish Reubens

1 package (15 ounces) frozen fish sticks (20)
1 can (16 ounces) sauerkraut
   Tartar sauce
6 slices rye bread
1 cup shredded Swiss cheese (about 4
   ounces)
   Whole pickled beets

Heat oven to 425°. Bake fish sticks as directed on package. Snip sauerkraut finely with scissors. Heat to boiling; drain. Spread tartar sauce over 1 side of each bread slice. Place 3 or 4 fish sticks on each slice; spread with tartar sauce. Top with sauerkraut and cheese. Bake on ungreased baking sheet until cheese is melted, about 5 minutes. Garnish with pickled beets.　　6 OPEN-FACE SANDWICHES.

Tuna-Corn Bake

1 can (10¾ ounces) condensed cream of
    chicken soup
1 can (9¼ ounces) tuna, drained and flaked
1 can (8 ounces) stewed tomatoes (reserve
    3 tomato pieces)
1 cup coarsely crumbled corn chips
½ small green pepper, chopped (about ¼
    cup)
2 teaspoons instant minced onion
½ teaspoon chili powder
    Dash of garlic salt
1 cup shredded Cheddar cheese (about 4
    ounces)
1 cup coarsely crumbled corn chips
    Chili sauce (optional)

Heat oven to 350°. Mix soup, tuna, tomatoes, 1 cup corn
chips, the green pepper, onion, chili powder and garlic salt
in greased 1½-quart casserole. Sprinkle with cheese and
arrange reserved tomato pieces in center. Sprinkle 1 cup
corn chips around tomatoes. Bake uncovered until bubbly,
about 30 minutes. Serve with chili sauce.   8 SERVINGS.

Mix ingredients in the casserole in which they will bake.

Sprinkle with cheese; add reserved tomato and chips.

Toss tuna, celery, mayonnaise, parsley and lemon juice.

Add croutons to chilled tuna mixture just before serving.

Tuna Toss

- 2 cans (6½ ounces each) tuna, chilled, drained and broken into chunks
- 2 medium stalks celery, sliced (about 1 cup)
- ½ to ⅔ cup mayonnaise or salad dressing
- ¼ cup snipped parsley
- 1 teaspoon lemon juice
- 6 cherry tomatoes
- 2 ounces brick or Cheddar cheese, cut into six ½-inch cubes
- 6 pimiento-stuffed olives
- 2 cups garlic-and-onion-flavored croutons
- 6 lettuce cups

Toss tuna, celery, mayonnaise, parsley and lemon juice; refrigerate 1 hour. Skewer tomatoes, cheese and olives on wooden picks. Toss croutons with tuna mixture; spoon into lettuce cups. Garnish with kabobs.   6 SERVINGS.

17

Tuna-Lemon Puff

2 slices white bread, torn into ¼-inch pieces (about 2 cups)
1 cup shredded Cheddar cheese (about 4 ounces)
1 can (6½ ounces) tuna, drained and flaked
¾ cup milk
3 eggs, separated
Grated peel of 1 medium lemon (optional)
1 tablespoon lemon juice
1 teaspoon instant minced onion
½ teaspoon salt
¼ teaspoon dry mustard
3 tablespoons butter or margarine, melted
½ teaspoon poppy seed

Heat oven to 350°. Mix 1½ cups of the bread, the cheese, tuna, milk, egg yolks, lemon peel, lemon juice, onion, salt and mustard. Beat egg whites until stiff but not dry; fold into tuna mixture. Pour into greased 1-quart casserole. Toss remaining bread, the butter and poppy seed; sprinkle over casserole. Bake uncovered until golden and set in center, about 40 minutes. Garnish with parsley.
6 SERVINGS.

LEMON-AID

If your recipe calls for lemon peel and juice, always grate the peel first, then squeeze the juice. Remove only the outer colored layer using quick downward strokes on the grater. Citrus fruits at room temperature yield more juice than when taken directly from the refrigerator. Rolling the fruit before juicing also helps.

Tuna Bake

7 ounces uncooked spaghetti
1 jar (5 ounces) pasteurized process cheese
  spread with bacon
2 cans (6½ ounces each) tuna, drained and
  flaked
1 medium stalk celery, sliced (about ½ cup)
2 tablespoons dried parsley flakes
1 cup milk
2 eggs, beaten
  Paprika

Heat oven to 375°. Break spaghetti into 2-inch pieces; prepare as directed on package. Drain. Toss spaghetti and
cheese spread. Stir in tuna, celery and parsley; pour into
greased 2-quart casserole. Mix milk and eggs; pour on
tuna-spaghetti mixture. Sprinkle with paprika. Bake uncovered until set, 30 to 35 minutes.   6 OR 7 SERVINGS.

Tuna Niçoise

½ cup French salad dressing
1 can (16 ounces) cut green beans, drained
1 can (8 ounces) whole new potatoes, sliced
2 heads Bibb or Boston lettuce
3 medium tomatoes, sliced
¼ teaspoon salt
2 cans (6½ ounces each) tuna, chilled,
  drained and broken into chunks
⅓ cup sliced pitted ripe olives

Pour dressing on beans and potatoes; refrigerate 1 hour.
Arrange lettuce leaves on each of 6 salad plates; add
tomato slices. Sprinkle with salt and top with tuna. Spoon
bean-potato mixture onto tuna. Garnish with olives.
6 OR 7 SERVINGS.

Stir pimiento cheese spread into hot drained macaroni until the cheese is melted.

Add part of the olives, the tuna, celery, mayonnaise, lemon juice and seasoned salt.

To make biscuits, sprinkle half of the crushed cereal over half the butter in pan.

Drop dough onto cereal in pan; drizzle with remaining butter. Add remaining cereal.

Tuna Salad with Biscuits

7 ounces uncooked elbow macaroni (about
  2 cups)
1 jar (8 ounces) pasteurized process
  pimiento cheese spread
1 jar (2 ounces) broken pimiento-stuffed
  olives, drained
2 cans (6½ ounces each) tuna, drained and
  broken into chunks
2 medium stalks celery, sliced (about 1 cup)
⅓ cup mayonnaise or salad dressing
2 teaspoons lemon juice
½ teaspoon seasoned salt
  Dried parsley flakes
  Corn Flake Biscuits (below)

Cook macaroni as directed on package; drain. Stir in cheese until melted. Reserve 2 tablespoons olives. Stir remaining olives, the tuna, celery, mayonnaise, lemon juice and seasoned salt into macaroni. Cover and refrigerate 2 hours. Garnish with reserved olives and parsley flakes. Serve with Corn Flake Biscuits.   6 SERVINGS.

CORN FLAKE BISCUITS
¼ cup butter or margarine, melted
1 cup crushed corn flake cereal (about 1¾
  cups uncrushed)
2 cups biscuit baking mix
½ cup cold water

Heat oven to 425°. Spread half of the butter in baking pan, 9x9x2 inches; sprinkle with half of the cereal. Stir baking mix and water until a soft dough forms; beat vigorously 20 strokes. Drop dough by tablespoonfuls onto cereal; drizzle with remaining butter. Press remaining cereal into dough. Bake until light brown, 12 to 15 minutes.

Seafaring Hero

- 1 loaf (1 pound) French bread
  Soft butter or margarine
- 2 packages (3 ounces each) cream cheese, softened
- ½ cup chopped pimiento-stuffed olives
- ½ to 1 teaspoon anchovy paste
- 2 cans (6½ ounces each) tuna, drained and flaked
- 1 medium cucumber, chopped (about ⅔ cup)
- ⅓ cup mayonnaise or salad dressing
- 1½ teaspoons lemon juice
- ¼ teaspoon onion salt

Cut loaf lengthwise into 3 layers; spread each layer with butter. Mix cheese, olives and anchovy paste; spread over bottom layer of bread. Mix remaining ingredients; spread over middle layer. Assemble sandwich; wrap and refrigerate. Just before serving, cut into 1-inch slices.

8 SERVINGS.

Tuna Heroes

6 Kaiser rolls, split and buttered
  Mayonnaise or salad dressing
6 lettuce leaves
1 can (6½ ounces) tuna, drained and flaked
1 medium stalk celery, chopped (about ½
  cup)
3 tablespoons mayonnaise or salad dressing
2 tablespoons chopped dill pickle
  Dash of onion salt
6 tablespoons bacon-flavored vegetable
  protein chips (optional)
1 large tomato, cut into 6 slices
6 slices process American cheese
6 pimiento-stuffed olives

Spread rolls with mayonnaise; place lettuce on bottom halves. Mix tuna, celery, 3 tablespoons mayonnaise, the pickle and onion salt; spread over lettuce. Top each with 1 tablespoon protein chips, a tomato slice and a cheese slice; cover with top of roll. Secure with wooden picks; garnish with olives.   6 SERVINGS.

Salmon Quiches

1 package (11 ounces) pie crust mix or
   sticks
1 can (about 16 ounces) salmon, drained
   and flaked
4 green onions, chopped (about 6
   tablespoons)
8 eggs
4 cups whipping cream or light cream (20%)
1½ teaspoons salt
 ½ teaspoon sugar
 ¼ teaspoon cayenne red pepper

Prepare pastry for two One-Crust Pies as directed on package. Divide salmon and onions between pastry-lined pie plates (see Timing Tip).

Beat eggs slightly; beat in whipping cream, salt, sugar and red pepper (see Timing Tip).

Heat oven to 425°. Pour half of the egg mixture on salmon and onions in each pie plate. Bake 15 minutes. Reduce oven temperature to 300° and bake until knife inserted 1 inch from edge comes out clean, about 45 minutes. Let stand 10 minutes before cutting.   12 SERVINGS.

Timing Tip: At this point, ingredients can be covered and refrigerated up to 24 hours. If you want to serve at different times, you can assemble ingredients ahead, then bake Salmon Quiches as needed.

Divide salmon and onions between two pastry-lined pie plates; cover and refrigerate.

Cover egg mixture and refrigerate. For split shifts, assemble and bake quiches as needed.

Drop the salmon mixture onto a hot griddle; flatten slightly.

Cook until cakes are golden brown, about 3 minutes; turn.

Salmon-Corn Cakes

3 eggs
2 tablespoons flour
2 teaspoons lemon juice
1 teaspoon salt
2 drops red pepper sauce
Dash of pepper
1 can (12 ounces) whole kernel corn, drained
1 can (7¾ ounces) salmon, drained and
flaked
Pimiento Sauce (right)

Grease heated griddle if necessary. Mix eggs, flour, lemon juice, salt, pepper sauce and pepper with hand beater until foamy. Stir in corn and salmon.

Drop mixture by generous ¼ cupfuls onto hot griddle; flatten slightly. Cook until golden brown, about 3 minutes on each side. Grease griddle as necessary. Serve corn cakes with Pimiento Sauce.   4 SERVINGS.

PIMIENTO SAUCE

½ cup dairy sour cream
¼ cup grated American cheese food
2 tablespoons chopped pimiento

Heat all ingredients just to boiling over low heat, stirring
constantly.

Spread butter mixture over bread. Arrange 6 slices bread in baking dish. Spread salmon mixture evenly over bread in dish.

Cut remaining bread diagonally in half; place on salmon mixture. Layer peas on bread. Pour soup mixture evenly on top.

Salmon Sandwich Bake

12 slices sandwich bread
¼ cup soft butter or margarine
2 teaspoons prepared mustard
2 cans (7¾ ounces each) red salmon,
    drained
1 cup shredded Cheddar cheese (about
    4 ounces)
¼ cup sliced pimiento-stuffed olives
1 small onion, chopped (about ¼ cup)
1 package (10 ounces) frozen green peas
1 can (10¾ ounces) condensed cream of
    shrimp soup
¼ cup milk
    Dill pickles

Toast bread; trim crusts. Mix butter and mustard; spread over 1 side of each bread slice. Arrange 6 slices bread buttered sides up in ungreased baking dish, 11¾ x 7½ x 1¾ inches.

Heat oven to 350°. Flake salmon, removing skin and bones. Mix salmon, cheese, olives and onion. Spread salmon mixture evenly over bread in baking dish. Cut remaining 6 slices bread diagonally in half; place buttered sides up on salmon mixture. Rinse frozen peas under running cold water to separate; layer on bread. Mix soup and milk; pour evenly on and around sandwiches. Bake uncovered until hot and bubbly, 25 to 30 minutes. Serve with dill pickles. 6 SERVINGS.

ARTICHOKE HEARTS are actually tiny whole artichokes which are canned and bottled before the thistle-like cores have toughened. On a fresh, mature artichoke the thistles are to be avoided; only the tender base of the artichoke leaves and the bottom layer beneath the core are edible — and delicious too!

Seafood Kabobs

Anchovy Sauce (right)
½ pound mushrooms
1 package (8 ounces) frozen cooked large shrimp, thawed
1 package (7 ounces) frozen breaded scallops, thawed
1 can (8½ ounces) artichoke hearts, drained and cut into fourths
1 medium green pepper, cut into 1-inch pieces (about 1 cup)
2 medium lemons, cut into eighths
½ teaspoon dried dill weed
3 to 4 cups hot cooked rice

Prepare Anchovy Sauce. Cut caps from mushrooms; reserve stems. Alternate shrimp, scallops, mushroom caps, artichoke hearts, green pepper pieces and lemon wedges on six 10- to 12-inch skewers as pictured.

Set oven control to broil and/or 550°. Brush Anchovy Sauce over kabobs. Broil with tops 3 to 4 inches from heat, brushing occasionally with sauce, until tender, 8 to 10 minutes.

Chop reserved mushroom stems. Heat stems, dill and rice in 2-quart saucepan over low heat, stirring occasionally, 5 minutes. Serve kabobs over rice; sprinkle with paprika if desired.   6 SERVINGS.

ANCHOVY SAUCE

Heat ⅓ cup butter or margarine, 1½ teaspoons anchovy paste, 1 teaspoon lemon juice and ¼ teaspoon onion juice, stirring constantly, until mixture is smooth.

Ahead of time, cook the rice and the mushrooms and prepare the shrimp mixture.

Transfer shrimp mixture to a chafing dish. Stir in mushrooms and wine; heat.

Shrimp and Artichokes au Vin

1 package (6 ounces) long-grain and wild
   rice
5 ounces mushrooms, sliced
¼ cup butter or margarine
3 tablespoons flour
½ teaspoon salt
¾ cup light cream (20%) or half-and-half
2 packages (6 ounces each) frozen cooked
   shrimp, thawed
2 jars (7 ounces each) marinated artichoke
   hearts, drained
¼ cup dry white wine
¼ cup grated Parmesan cheese

Prepare rice as directed on package. While rice is cooking, cook and stir mushrooms in butter until tender, 3 to 4 minutes. Remove mushrooms with slotted spoon; reserve. Stir flour and salt into butter. Cook, stirring constantly, until smooth and bubbly; remove from heat. Stir in cream. Heat to boiling, stirring constantly. Boil and stir 1 minute. Stir in shrimp and artichoke hearts; heat about 5 minutes.

Transfer shrimp mixture to chafing dish or skillet. Stir in mushrooms and wine; heat until hot. Sprinkle with cheese. Serve shrimp over rice.   6 SERVINGS.

Shrimp and Sprouts

½ pound mushrooms, sliced (about 3 cups)
2 green onions (with tops), sliced (about
  ¼ cup)
1 clove garlic, finely chopped
2 tablespoons vegetable oil
1 package (10 ounces) frozen French-style
  green beans
1 can (16 ounces) bean sprouts, rinsed and
  drained*
1 package (8 ounces) frozen cooked large
  shrimp, thawed
1 cup water
1½ teaspoons salt
1 teaspoon instant chicken bouillon
½ teaspoon ground ginger
¼ cup water
2 tablespoons cornstarch
3 cups hot cooked rice

Cook and stir mushrooms, onions and garlic in oil in 10-inch skillet until onion is tender, about 5 minutes.

Rinse frozen beans under running cold water to separate. Stir beans, bean sprouts, shrimp, 1 cup water, the salt, instant bouillon and ginger into mushrooms. Heat to boiling; reduce heat. Cover and simmer 10 minutes.

Mix ¼ cup water and the cornstarch; stir into shrimp mixture. Heat to boiling, stirring constantly. Boil and stir 1 minute. Serve over rice.   6 SERVINGS.

*4 cups cooked fresh bean sprouts can be substituted for the canned bean sprouts.

For 3 cups of rice, heat 2 cups water, 1 cup rice and 1 teaspoon salt to boiling; stir twice.

Reduce heat to simmer. Cover pan tightly; cook 14 minutes. (Do not lift cover or stir.)

Remove the pan of hot rice from the heat. Do not drain. Fluff rice lightly with fork.

Then cover the rice again and let it steam, without stirring, for 5 to 10 minutes.

Shrimp Cantonese

   1 cup uncooked regular rice
   ¼ cup sugar
   2 tablespoons cornstarch
   1 can (13½ ounces) pineapple chunks,
      drained (reserve syrup)
   ¼ cup vinegar
   2 teaspoons soy sauce
   2 medium stalks celery, chopped (about
      1 cup)
   4 green onions (with tops), sliced (about
      ½ cup)
   ½ medium green pepper, cut into ¼-inch
      strips
   1 large tomato, cut into eighths
   2 cans (4½ ounces each) jumbo shrimp,
      drained
1½ cups shredded Swiss cheese (about 6
      ounces)
   ⅓ cup toasted sliced almonds

Cook rice as directed on package. Mix sugar and cornstarch in 3-quart saucepan. Add enough water to reserved
pineapple syrup to measure 1 cup. Stir pineapple liquid,
vinegar and soy sauce into sugar mixture gradually. Cook
over medium heat, stirring constantly, until mixture thick-
ens and boils. Boil and stir 1 minute.

Stir pineapple, celery, onions and green pepper into sauce
mixture. Fold in tomato and shrimp. Heat until shrimp is
hot. Toss cheese and rice; pack into buttered 4-cup mold.
Immediately invert on large serving plate. Top with shrimp
mixture; sprinkle with almonds.   6 TO 8 SERVINGS.

Prepare the vegetables while the rice is cooking.

Add fruit, vegetables and shrimp to the sauce.

Toss the cheese and rice; pack into 4-cup mold.

Invert mold on serving plate; top with shrimp mixture.

Shrimp Curry

1 small onion, chopped (about ¼ cup)
1 small apple, chopped (about ½ cup)
¼ cup butter or margarine
1 can (10¾ ounces) condensed cream of
    chicken soup
½ cup milk
2 to 3 teaspoons curry powder
1 teaspoon ground ginger
1 teaspoon salt
2 tablespoons plum jam
1 tablespoon lemon juice
2 cups fresh or frozen shrimp, cleaned and
    cooked
1 small cucumber, pared and cut into cubes
    (about ¾ cup)
2 cups hot cooked rice
    Condiments (below)

Cook and stir onion and apple in butter in 10-inch skillet over medium heat until onion is tender. Mix soup, milk, curry powder, ginger and salt; stir into onion and apple. Cook and stir over low heat until hot and bubbly, about 4 minutes.

Mix jam and lemon juice until smooth; stir into soup mixture. Stir in shrimp and cucumber. Heat 3 minutes. Serve with rice and Condiments.   4 TO 6 SERVINGS.

CONDIMENTS

Serve the following in ramekins or custard cups: chopped peanuts, chutney, coconut, raisins, chopped green pepper, India relish and chopped hard-cooked eggs.

Crabmeat Curry: Substitute crabmeat (cartilage removed), cut into 1-inch pieces, for the shrimp.

Curry comes from the Hindu *Kari* and means "spiced food."

CHIVES, like shallots, have a delicate onion flavor with little aftertaste. Use them instead of onions for variety and color. The clover-like blossoms make pretty garnishes too. Chives can be frozen to use year round.

Rice-Shrimp Pie

6 eggs
½ cup uncooked instant rice
½ cup water
2 teaspoons snipped chives
½ teaspoon salt
¼ teaspoon garlic salt
¼ teaspoon ground ginger
1 can (4½ ounces) deveined small shrimp,
    rinsed and drained
Paprika
Lemon-Tomato Sauce (below)

Heat oven to 350°. Beat eggs with fork until foamy. Stir in rice, water, chives, salt, garlic salt and ginger; pour into greased 9-inch pie plate. Arrange shrimp on egg mixture; sprinkle with paprika.

Bake uncovered until knife inserted near center comes out clean, about 30 minutes. Serve with Lemon-Tomato Sauce.
4 SERVINGS.

LEMON-TOMATO SAUCE
Heat ½ cup condensed tomato soup, ½ teaspoon lemon juice and ¼ teaspoon salt to boiling, stirring occasionally.

Cook and stir celery in butter until the celery is tender.

Stir in soup, crabmeat, sour cream, lemon peel and bitters.

Crabby Joes

- 2 medium stalks celery, chopped (about 1 cup)
- 1 tablespoon butter or margarine
- 1 can (10¾ ounces) condensed cream of shrimp soup
- 2 cans (7½ ounces each) crabmeat, drained and flaked*
- ½ cup dairy sour cream
- 1 tablespoon grated lemon peel
  Dash of aromatic bitters
- 4 English muffins, split and toasted
  Paprika

Cook and stir celery in butter in 10-inch skillet until celery is tender, about 5 minutes. Stir in soup, crabmeat, sour cream, lemon peel and bitters. Heat just to boiling. Serve over hot muffins; sprinkle with paprika.   4 SERVINGS.

*1 can (7 ounces) fish flakes, drained, can be substituted for 1 can of the crabmeat.

Crab Scramble

¼ cup butter or margarine
12 eggs
½ cup milk
 1 teaspoon salt
½ teaspoon white pepper
½ teaspoon dried dill weed
 1 can (7½ ounces) crabmeat, rinsed and
     drained
 1 package (8 ounces) cream cheese, cut up
     Paprika

Heat oven to 350°. Heat butter in baking dish, 8x8x2 inches, in oven until melted. Tilt dish until bottom is coated.

Beat eggs, milk, salt, pepper and dill until fluffy. Stir in crabmeat and cheese; pour into baking dish. Sprinkle with paprika. Bake until set in center, 40 to 45 minutes.
9 SERVINGS.

Heat butter in baking dish, 8x8x2 inches. Tilt to coat the bottom of the dish.

Beat eggs, milk, salt, pepper and dill weed. Stir in crabmeat and cream cheese.

Pour beaten eggs over mushrooms while sauce simmers.

Sprinkle omelet with cheese and bake 5 minutes.

Mushroom Omelet

Asparagus-Cheese Sauce (below)
1 cup sliced mushrooms
2 tablespoons butter or margarine
8 eggs, beaten
1 teaspoon salt
¼ teaspoon pepper
⅓ cup grated Parmesan cheese

Prepare Asparagus-Cheese Sauce. Heat oven to 450°. Cook and stir mushrooms in butter in 10-inch ovenproof omelet pan or skillet over medium heat until tender. Mix eggs, salt and pepper; pour on mushrooms.

As mixture begins to set at bottom and side, gently lift cooked portion with spatula so thin uncooked portion can flow to bottom. Cook until eggs are set, about 5 minutes. Sprinkle omelet with cheese. Bake 5 minutes. Let stand 1 minute before cutting into wedges. Top each serving with about ½ cup of the sauce.   6 SERVINGS.

ASPARAGUS-CHEESE SAUCE

Mix 1 can (11 ounces) condensed Cheddar cheese soup and ½ cup water in 2-quart saucepan. Stir in 1 package (10 ounces) frozen cut asparagus, partially thawed. Heat to boiling; reduce heat. Simmer uncovered, stirring occasionally, until asparagus is tender.

Eggs in a Ring

1 egg
1 cup milk
¼ cup vegetable oil
1 cup all-purpose flour
1 cup whole wheat flour
1 cup shredded Cheddar cheese (about
   4 ounces)
2 tablespoons sugar
1 tablespoon baking powder
½ teaspoon salt
Creamed Eggs (right)

Heat oven to 400°. Grease 6-cup ring mold. Beat egg; stir in milk and oil. Stir in flours, cheese, sugar, baking powder and salt just until flour is moistened. (Batter will be lumpy.) Spoon into mold. Bake until golden brown, 20 to 25 minutes; unmold. Prepare Creamed Eggs; serve in center of hot muffin ring.   6 SERVINGS.

Mix the batter just to moisten flour. Batter will be lumpy.

Spoon batter into greased ring mold; bake until golden brown.

To prepare Creamed Eggs, heat frozen peas and chicken soup.

Fold in the remaining ingredients. Simmer 3 to 5 minutes.

CREAMED EGGS

- 1 package (10 ounces) frozen green peas
- 1 can (10¾ ounces) condensed cream of chicken soup
- 3 hard-cooked eggs, sliced
- 6 to 8 pimiento-stuffed olives, sliced
- 2 tablespoons chopped onion
- ⅛ teaspoon poultry seasoning

Heat frozen peas and soup in 2-quart saucepan over medium heat, stirring occasionally. Fold in eggs, olives, onion and poultry seasoning; reduce heat. Simmer uncovered 3 to 5 minutes.

Break each egg into measuring cup or saucer; slip into skillet. Cook until whites are set.

Add salt and pepper, water, cheese, oregano and paprika. Cover; let stand 5 minutes.

Mozzarella Eggs

1 tablespoon butter or margarine
4 eggs
½ teaspoon salt
  Dash of pepper
1½ teaspoons water
4 slices mozzarella cheese
½ teaspoon dried oregano leaves
  Paprika

Heat butter in 10-inch skillet until just hot enough to sizzle a drop of water. Break each egg into measuring cup or saucer; carefully slip eggs one at a time into skillet. Cook eggs over low heat until whites are set; sprinkle with salt and pepper.

Pour water into skillet. Place a cheese slice on each egg; sprinkle with oregano and paprika. Remove from heat. Cover and let stand 5 minutes before serving. 4 SERVINGS.

EGGS-PERT ADVICE

Store eggs in the refrigerator up to 1 week. Keep them insulated in their original carton (saves flavor) with the large ends up to hold the yolks in the centers.

Leftover egg whites can be refrigerated covered up to 10 days. Leftover yolks should be covered with water in a closed container and refrigerated up to 3 days.

Eggs separate best when they are cold, but beat faster and lighter when they are at room temperature; so separate them first and then let them stand 1 hour before beating.

Sprinkle toast with 1 cup of the cheese; add asparagus.

Pour on seasoned custard; top with paprika. Refrigerate.

Cheese Bake

6 slices white bread, toasted
2 tablespoons butter or margarine, softened
2 cups shredded Swiss cheese (about 8 ounces)
1 package (10 ounces) frozen asparagus cuts, cooked and drained
2 cups milk
4 eggs, slightly beaten
2 tablespoons snipped parsley
1 teaspoon salt
1 teaspoon Worcestershire sauce
½ teaspoon dry mustard
¼ to ½ teaspoon red pepper sauce
¼ teaspoon paprika

Spread 1 side of each toast slice with butter; cut crosswise into thirds. Arrange 9 toast pieces, buttered sides up, in ungreased baking dish, 10x6x1¾ inches. Sprinkle with 1 cup of the cheese; top with asparagus. Sprinkle remaining cheese over asparagus. Top with remaining toast pieces, buttered sides down.

Mix milk, eggs, parsley, salt, Worcestershire sauce, mustard and pepper sauce until smooth; pour on toast. Sprinkle with paprika. Cover and refrigerate 4 to 6 hours.

Heat oven to 325°. Bake uncovered until knife inserted halfway between center and edge comes out clean, about 1 hour 15 minutes. Garnish with parsley.   6 SERVINGS.

One more way to enjoy Swiss cheese.

Cheese-Fruit Mold

2½ cups boiling water
1 package (6 ounces) orange-flavored gelatin*
½ cup sugar
1 package (8 ounces) cream cheese, softened
2 cans (13¼ ounces each) crushed pineapple
2 cups shredded Cheddar cheese (about 8 ounces)
2 cups creamed cottage cheese
2 teaspoons lemon juice
Salad greens
Honey Dressing (below)
Crackers

Pour boiling water on gelatin and sugar in large bowl; stir until gelatin and sugar are dissolved. Beat in cream cheese until smooth. Stir in pineapple (with syrup), Cheddar cheese, cottage cheese and lemon juice. Pour into 12-cup mold. Refrigerate until firm, about 8 hours. Unmold on salad greens and serve with Honey Dressing and crackers. 10 SERVINGS.

*Lime-flavored gelatin can be substituted for the orange-flavored gelatin.

HONEY DRESSING
Mix 2 cups unflavored yogurt and ½ cup honey. Sprinkle with ground nutmeg.

Beat the cream cheese into the gelatin mixture until smooth.

Stir in pineapple (with syrup), remaining cheeses and juice.

Broccoli-Cheese Pie

    6 cups water
    1 teaspoon salt
    3 ounces uncooked macaroni rings (about
        ¾ cup)
    1 egg yolk
    1 tablespoon snipped chives
    1 cup shredded Cheddar cheese (about
        4 ounces)
    1 package (10 ounces) frozen chopped
        broccoli
    ½ teaspoon salt
    4 eggs
    1 egg white
    1 cup creamed cottage cheese
    1 tablespoon snipped chives
    1 teaspoon salt
        Paprika

Heat oven to 375°. Heat water and 1 teaspoon salt to boiling; stir in macaroni. Boil until tender, 5 to 8 minutes. Drain; rinse in cold water.

Beat egg yolk; stir in macaroni and 1 tablespoon chives. Press mixture against bottom and side of greased 9-inch pie plate with back of spoon. Bake 10 minutes; remove from oven. Cool 10 minutes.

Increase oven temperature to 425°. Sprinkle Cheddar cheese over crust. Prepare broccoli as directed on package, using ½ teaspoon salt; drain. Arrange broccoli on cheese. Beat eggs, egg white, cottage cheese, 1 tablespoon chives and 1 teaspoon salt; pour on broccoli. Sprinkle with paprika.

Bake uncovered 15 minutes. Reduce oven temperature to 300°. Bake until knife inserted 1 inch from edge comes out clean, about 30 minutes. Cool 10 minutes before serving. 6 SERVINGS.

Stir the cooked macaroni and chives into the egg yolk.

Press the macaroni mixture in greased 9-inch pie plate.

Sprinkle cheese over crust; top with hot cooked broccoli.

Pour egg mixture on broccoli; sprinkle with paprika.

Spaghetti-Bean Sprouts Salad

    7 ounces uncooked vermicelli
   ¾ cup mayonnaise or salad dressing
    1 tablespoon soy sauce
    1 teaspoon salt
    1 teaspoon prepared mustard
   ¼ teaspoon garlic powder
       Dash of white pepper
    1 can (16 ounces) bean sprouts, drained
    1 can (3 ounces) sliced mushrooms, drained
    1 medium stalk celery, sliced (about ½ cup)
   ⅓ medium green pepper, chopped (about ⅓
          cup)
    1 small onion, chopped (about ¼ cup)
    1 cup frozen green peas
   ½ cup cashews or peanuts, coarsely chopped
          (optional)
       Spinach leaves
       Sliced radishes or tomatoes

Break vermicelli into 2-inch pieces; cook as directed on package. Rinse under running cold water; drain.

Mix mayonnaise, soy sauce, salt, mustard, garlic powder and white pepper in large bowl. Stir in vermicelli, bean sprouts, mushrooms, celery, green pepper and onion. Rinse peas under running cold water to separate. Stir into salad. Refrigerate at least 3 hours.

Stir in cashews. Serve in bowl lined with spinach leaves; garnish with radishes.   8 SERVINGS.

Break vermicelli into pieces.

Rinse under cold water; drain.

Mix the mayonnaise and seasonings in a large bowl.

Stir in the vermicelli and all vegetables; refrigerate.

Harvest Spaghetti

- 1 can (28 ounces) whole tomatoes
- 1 can (15 ounces) tomato sauce
- 1 can (4 ounces) mushroom stems and pieces
- 3 medium zucchini (about 1 pound), cut into ½-inch cubes
- 2 medium stalks celery, chopped (about 1 cup)
- 3 tablespoons instant minced onion
- 2 teaspoons dried marjoram leaves
- 1 teaspoon sugar
- ¾ teaspoon salt
- ¼ teaspoon garlic salt
- ½ cup grated Parmesan cheese
- 7 to 8 ounces uncooked spaghetti

Heat tomatoes (with liquid), tomato sauce, mushrooms (with liquid), zucchini, celery, onion, marjoram, sugar, salt and garlic salt to boiling in Dutch oven; reduce heat. Cover and simmer 45 minutes, stirring occasionally. Stir in ¼ cup of the cheese.

Cook spaghetti as directed on package; drain. Pour zucchini mixture on hot spaghetti. Serve with remaining cheese and garnish with parsley.   4 SERVINGS.

MEATLESS MAINSTAYS

About ¼ of the average daily protein requirement is supplied by 1/5 pound of boneless meat, poultry or fish; **or** ¼ pound with some bone; **or** 2½ large eggs; **or** 1¾ cups milk or buttermilk; **or** two 1-ounce slices of American or Swiss cheese; **or** ½ cup cottage cheese; **or** ¼ cup peanut butter or vegetable protein chips.

You can stir the macaroni into 6 cups boiling salted water and cook and stir 3 minutes.

Remove from heat; cover tightly. Let stand 10 minutes. (It cooks as it stands.)

Tomato-Cheese Macaroni

7 ounces uncooked macaroni (about 2 cups)
1 medium green pepper, chopped
4 green onions (with tops), sliced (about ½ cup)
2 tablespoons vegetable oil
1 can (16 ounces) whole tomatoes
1 can (8 ounces) tomato sauce
¼ teaspoon pepper
3 cups shredded process American cheese

Heat oven to 350°. Cook macaroni as directed on package; drain. Pour hot macaroni into ungreased 2-quart casserole. Reserve 3 tablespoons chopped green pepper. Cook and stir remaining green pepper and the onions in oil in 2-quart saucepan until onions are tender, about 5 minutes. Stir in tomatoes (with liquid), tomato sauce and pepper; break up tomatoes with fork. Heat until tomatoes are hot; pour on hot macaroni.

Stir 2½ cups of the cheese into macaroni mixture. Bake uncovered 25 minutes. Sprinkle with remaining cheese; bake uncovered until cheese is melted, about 5 minutes. Garnish with reserved green pepper.   6 SERVINGS.

Meatless Lasagne

Lasagne Sauce (right)
2 cartons (12 ounces each) creamed
   cottage cheese (small curd)
1 cup grated Parmesan cheese
1 tablespoon dried parsley flakes
2 teaspoons salt
1½ teaspoons dried oregano leaves
8 ounces uncooked lasagne noodles
3 cups shredded mozzarella cheese

Prepare Lasagne Sauce. Mix cottage cheese, ½ cup of the Parmesan cheese, the parsley, salt and oregano; reserve. Cook noodles as directed on package; drain.

Heat oven to 350°. Reserve ½ cup sauce. Layer ⅓ each of the noodles, remaining sauce, mozzarella cheese and cottage cheese mixture in ungreased lasagne pan, 14x8x2 inches, or baking pan, 13x9x2 inches. Repeat 2 times. Top with reserved sauce; sprinkle with remaining Parmesan cheese. Bake uncovered 45 minutes. Let stand 15 minutes. 12 SERVINGS.

Layer ⅓ of the hot noodles in ungreased lasagne pan.

Reserve ½ cup sauce. Pour on ⅓ of the remaining sauce.

Add ⅓ each of the mozzarella cheese and cheese mixture.

Repeat layers 2 times. Add reserved sauce and cheese.

LASAGNE SAUCE

2 cans (15 ounces each) tomato sauce
1 can (16 ounces) whole tomatoes (with liquid)
3 cans (4 ounces each) mushroom stems and pieces (with liquid)
1 medium onion, chopped (about ½ cup)
2 tablespoons sugar
2 tablespoons dried parsley flakes
1 teaspoon salt
1 teaspoon dried basil leaves
1 clove garlic, finely chopped

Heat all ingredients to boiling, stirring occasionally; reduce heat. Simmer uncovered 45 minutes.

For Peanut Soup, chop ½ cup peanuts in blender; reserve.

Blend remaining peanuts, milk and soup until smooth; heat.

To make pizzas, spread the muffins with peanut butter and applesauce. Top with peanuts.

Top each half with a cheese slice; sprinkle with vegetable protein chips and broil.

Peanut Soup

 cup salted peanuts
 cup skim milk
 can (10¾ ounces) condensed cream of
   celery soup
 jar (4 ounces) sliced pimiento, drained
 teaspoon aromatic bitters

Place ½ cup of the peanuts in blender container. Cover
and blend on high speed until chopped, 8 to 10 seconds;
pour into bowl and reserve. Place remaining peanuts, the
milk and soup in blender container. Cover and blend on
high speed until smooth, about 1 minute. Pour into 1-quart
saucepan. Stir in pimiento and bitters. Heat to boiling,
stirring constantly. Sprinkle with reserved peanuts.
5 SERVINGS.

Peanut Pizzas

 4 English muffins, split and toasted
 ½ cup peanut butter
 ½ cup applesauce*
 3 tablespoons chopped peanuts
 8 slices pasteurized process Swiss cheese
 3 tablespoons bacon-flavored vegetable
     protein chips

Spread cut sides of muffin halves with peanut butter, then
with applesauce; sprinkle with peanuts. Top each muffin
half with cheese slice; sprinkle with protein chips.

Set oven control to broil and/or 550°. Broil with tops 4 to
5 inches from heat until cheese is melted and pizzas are
hot, 1 to 2 minutes.   4 SERVINGS.

*½ cup honey or grape jelly can be substituted for the
applesauce.

Reserve some green pepper for garnish; cook remainder in butter until tender.

Stir in beans (with liquid), cheese and chili powder. Cook until cheese is melted.

Beany Rarebit

- 1 **small green pepper, chopped (about ½ cup)**
- 2 **tablespoons butter or margarine**
- 1 **can (16 ounces) kidney beans**
- 2 **cups shredded American cheese (about 8 ounces)**
- ½ **teaspoon chili powder**
- 6 **hard rolls**

Reserve 2 tablespoons green pepper. Cook and stir remaining green pepper in butter in 2-quart saucepan until tender, about 5 minutes. Stir in beans (with liquid), cheese and chili powder. Cook over low heat, stirring occasionally until cheese is melted, about 5 minutes. Split rolls; serve rarebit over rolls. Garnish with reserved green pepper.
4 TO 6 SERVINGS.

Crunchy Baked Soybeans

12 ounces dried soybeans (about 2 cups)
 6 cups water
 1 teaspoon salt
½ cup bacon-flavored vegetable protein chips
⅓ cup packed brown sugar
¼ cup molasses
 1 medium onion, chopped (about ½ cup)
 1 teaspoon salt
 1 teaspoon dry mustard
 1 can (15 ounces) tomato sauce

Heat soybeans, water and 1 teaspoon salt to boiling; boil 2 minutes. Remove from heat. Cover and let stand 1 hour. Drain soybeans, reserving ¾ cup liquid.

Heat oven to 325°. Mix soybeans, reserved bean liquid, protein chips, brown sugar, molasses, onion, 1 teaspoon salt and the mustard. Pour into ungreased 1½-quart casserole. Cover and bake 3 hours. Stir in tomato sauce; bake 1 hour.   6 SERVINGS.

SOYBEANS contain 1½ times as much protein as other dried beans, and that protein is high quality. Use as meat substitutes and extenders. Store and soak as you would other dried beans, but expect them to be firmer after cooking. Add acid foods after beans are tender. One cup dried yields 2½ cups cooked.

EGGS are an excellent source of complete protein. Their sizes are based on the weight per dozen: Jumbo (30 ounces), Extra Large (27 ounces), Large (24 ounces—this is the size used in most recipe testing), Medium (21 ounces), Small (18 ounces) and Peewee (15 ounces). The price of eggs is determined by quality and size.

Calico Rice Bake

     4 eggs
     1 package (10 ounces) frozen mixed
        vegetables, thawed
  2½ cups cooked rice
     1 cup creamed cottage cheese (small curd)
   ½ cup grated Parmesan cheese
   ½ cup shredded sharp Cheddar cheese
        (about 2 ounces)
     1 small onion, chopped (about ¼ cup)
   ½ teaspoon salt

Heat oven to 350°. Grease baking dish, 8x8x2 inches. Beat eggs; stir in remaining ingredients. Spread mixture in baking dish. Bake uncovered until set in center, 40 to 45 minutes.   6 SERVINGS.

The truth shattered her sanity...

Crystal couldn't remember anything about her emotional collapse. She only knew the police had discovered her in a park, unable to move or speak. Then her husband, Lorenzo, who had grown inexplicably aloof, arranged to have her committed to a mental institution.

For weeks she hovered on the brink of madness. Then, with sickening clarity, one fact became clear.

Lorenzo wanted her dead.

EXPERIENCE THE THRILL
OF LOVE...AND DANGER!

MYSTIQUE BOOKS bring you the thrill of suspense and romance in a breathless blend that will leave you eager for more.

MYSTIQUE BOOKS take you into a world where idyllic love is mysteriously threatened. You'll travel to such exotic places as the sunny Caribbean, romantic Paris, the white beaches of Cyprus or the intimidating streets of Istanbul. But wherever you go, romance proves to be a dangerous encounter.

You'll love these exciting, adventure-filled books. Each is an unforgettable reading experience. Four new titles are published every month. Look for them wherever paperback books are sold.

Island
of Fear

by DOMENICA

MYSTIQUE BOOKS

TORONTO • LONDON • NEW YORK
HAMBURG • AMSTERDAM • STOCKHOLM

ISLAND OF FEAR/first published November 1980

ISBN 0-373-50101-3

Chapter 1

A noise had awakened me; a gentle sound, as of someone placing a tray on a metal table. Yet it represented something I had no wish to face. I could ignore it for a time, that I knew from past experience, so I kept my eyes closed and struggled to return to my dream.

I had been on a beach—a wide, beautiful, Connecticut beach, with the waves washing peacefully against sun-bleached sand. Tufts of tall grass formed small hills that offered safety for sandpipers' nests. The sky was a perfect blue, with tiny white clouds forming shadow patterns that raced with me from the rocks that bordered the sand to the clear sparkle of the water.

I wasn't alone, that I knew, but my companion held himself apart, too involved in his game of hide-and-seek to notice my sudden fright. One shadow, and one shadow only, refused to join in the riotous rush into the sea. This dark shape hovered over me, blocking my view of the sun, isolating me from warmth and happiness.

"Mark?" I called out his name softly at first, not yet willing to let him know of my foolish fright. The shadow seemed to lengthen at the sound of my voice. Panic overwhelmed me. "Mark!" I shouted, and began to run wildly about, hoping to escape the menacing darkness. "Mark, I need you!"

He appeared abruptly, stepping from behind a mound of grass and sand like some rescuing angel, his arms outstretched. I saw him, and I ran. His arms closed around me, his lips pressed against mine, and somehow the shadow was gone.

And then the sound had wakened me. I wanted those arms to hold me again. I needed them! Only they could protect me from the madness that threatened to destroy me.

"I know you're awake, Mrs. Santos. It's a beautiful day. Imagine—the weatherman says we'll have no more rain until late this afternoon."

I opened my eyes reluctantly. Where was I? Not on my beach. Not where I wanted most to be. I seemed to be in a hospital bed, and a dark-haired nurse stood over me, a small paper cup in one hand, a plastic container of pills in the other.

I had struggled with just such an awakening before. I had accepted the proffered medicine, smiled patiently as the nurse smoothed out my bed, and then I had dropped off again into the half world of dreams.

This time it was different. The nurse smiled gently as she waited for me to prop up my head. "You're doing better. Your sleep was less troubled. The doctor has said we don't need the drug today." She dropped the pills into my hand. "Now, isn't that nice?"

She waited while I put the medicine into my mouth and washed it down with the water. "Let me help you sit up. I'm so glad the sun is shining! And the buds are beginning to show on the trees in the park across the road." She fluffed my pillows and half lifted me into a sitting position. Then she strode swiftly across the room to the window. I heard her skirt swish as she moved, and I wondered if that sound had inspired my dream of the ocean.

The light startled me when it spilled onto my bed. It was too bright, too filled with untapped energy. Instinctively I brought my arm up to shield my eyes. The nurse saw my action and closed the blinds halfway. "Is that better? Good! Now just rest awhile. I'll be back to comb your hair and make you pretty for your visit."

She was gone before I was able to gather my thoughts. I stared at the door, overwhelmed by a great frustration. There were so many questions I needed to have answered. Where was I? I knew I was in some hospital, but where? What kind of hospital? And most of all—why was I here?

Until she returned I could get no explanations—unless my own mind provided them. But when I tried to prod my memory I felt the weakness returning. A sort of helplessness, as if something was holding the memories back.

I had other questions that were of importance, too. The nurse had called me Mrs. Santos. But the name sounded strange to me. And she had spoken of a visit. A visit from whom?

I stared at the park, searching idly for the budding branches the nurse had admired, but my thoughts were on my problems. Something had caused me to be brought to the hospital. Surely, even if I could not remember my own identity, I ought to remember why I was sick. I closed my eyes and let myself fall back into dreamland. There would be time for more answers. . . .

The soft touch of a hand on my wrist awakened me. Someone was checking my pulse. I opened my eyes and met the gaze of a kindly-faced, elderly man dressed in the white coat of a medical doctor. He smiled. "Good afternoon! Are you having trouble pulling out of the drug?"

I nodded.

"Any palpitations?"

I shook my head.

"Feel pretty good, then?"

"I think so. Dr. . . . ?"

"Shabib. You don't remember being introduced to me when you arrived?"

I felt suddenly guilty. "No. Should I? I don't remember very much." I clutched his arm in sudden panic. "What's the matter with me? Why can't I remember anything?"

He pried my fingers loose and gently lowered my arm to the bed. "Please, Mrs. Santos, don't let yourself get upset. What you are experiencing is perfectly normal. You've had a bad experience and your mind couldn't cope with the stress. Here with us you've had a period of respite, and now it's important that you not rush the return of your memory. Let it flow back slowly. You'll be able to take it if you don't try to rush things."

My memory of what? "Was I in an accident?"

He shook his head. "No, my dear. You sustained no injuries. In fact, you're a very healthy young lady. I gave you a Valium this morning, to take the edge off your nerves. Call the nurse if you need her—or if you get hungry." His eyes sparkled. "You are hungry, aren't you?"

I nodded. "I'm thirsty, too. The nurse gave me only a tiny glass of water."

"Good! I'll speak to Amelia. She'll help you get yourself fixed up, too. Mr. Santos phoned to say he'd be in this evening—late. Some business or other. You're fortunate to have such a fine husband. He'll be pleased to see you conscious for a change."

So . . . my expected visitor was Mr. Santos, my husband. At least one question had been answered. But why couldn't I picture him in my head? Was he the Mark to whom I had appealed in my dream? Was my husband the one who shielded me from terror?

"How long have I been . . . ?" I probed the kindly doctor further, almost dreading his answer.

"A few weeks . . . almost a month. Average for most of our patients." He glanced at the open drapes. "Is the light too bright?"

"No, it's fine, thank you."

"Well, then, just be patient for a few moments and you'll have breakfast. I'll drop by again, after visiting hours." He was out the door before I could stop him. Once more I was alone with my questions.

What answers had I? I needed, suddenly, to see my own face, but there was no mirror in sight. I studied my room more carefully. Both the doctor and the nurse had used the same door, obviously to enter the corridor that connected my room to the rest of the hospital. Another door remained shut. I got up to investigate.

At first I moved unsteadily, my knees threatening to buckle under me. But by the time I reached the end of my bed I was moving more easily. I caught the handle of the mystery door and pulled it open.

The room before me was not typical of any hospital I had ever known. The walls were covered with yellow silk paper. A pale pink and yellow rug covered the floor. The furniture was exquisite French Provincial, upholstered in fine brocade. A door at the far end of the room opened to a modern, luxurious bathroom with marble fixtures.

I stepped before the mirror and studied my face. The features that greeted me were pleasing, even to my critical eyes. My nose was straight and fine, a perfect match to my oval face. Eyes that were clear and blue, but troubled, stared back at me.

Stepping back, I studied my body. I was slender and tall—willowy, maybe. My hair was messed from sleep, but even uncombed it seemed to sparkle with health, as if someone had kept it brushed during my weeks of unconsciousness. It seemed to fall naturally over my right shoulder, as if it had been trained to do so. "My princess with the golden hair, lost in the wilderness . . . ."

Lorenzo had said that! My husband—Lorenzo Santos. I felt a glow of triumph. Things were coming back, as Shabib had said they would. Yet the memory brought me no comfort. It filled me instead with a vague uneasiness.

I shook my head impatiently. I'd never get anywhere if I let a feeling frighten me. So I was married to Lorenzo Santos. And I was . . . ? I stared again into the morror. I was . . . ?

Crystal Santos! It was as if a light had turned on in my head. I was Crystal Santos. Again the uneasy fear. Why did my own name frighten me? I leaned forward and stared into my reflection. I felt uneasy because my husband's name was not the same as that of the man in my dreams: Mark, whose comforting presence I had sought so urgently.

I shrugged. At least I had a name. I was making progress.

But why the fright? I tried again. "I am Crystal Santos, wife of Lorenzo Santos." My voice trembled. Something in the bare statement of fact caused the fear. Had Lorenzo hurt me? I shook my head. Dr. Shabib had said I had no injuries. But was he lying?

My fingers trembled as I removed my robe and white hospital gown and stood nude before the mirror. My body was firm and smooth. My skin was pale, but free of any blemishes. Someone once had told me I looked like the statue of the mermaid in the port of Copenhagen.

Someone? Most probably Lorenzo. But then why did the thought of him scare me so? No answer came, though I gazed long into the mirror. At last, depressed by my failure to learn more, I pulled on my gown.

"Does madam need any help? I've brought lunch." Amelia, the nurse, had returned. This time, however, I detected an accent in her voice. To my surprise, I knew her native tongue.

I reentered the white room in which I had awakened. "I was just saying hello to myself." I spoke in French. The words flowed easily. Was I French, too? No. I was American. But was I in Europe? If so— why?

I saw now that Amelia was a young woman, probably in her mid-twenties, with dark hair and smooth olive skin. She smiled as I entered. "Ah!" She reverted to French with obvious delight. "I am pleased you speak my language. I did not do so well in English classes."

"Do you have many American patients?"

She shrugged. "No, but there are some. This is a very expensive hospital, and Dr. Shabib is an authority in his field. People come from all over the world for treatment. Of course," she went on, eager to chat, "our medical facilities have a good reputation, as well, and we do have some chronic-care patients and others that come for postoperative attention . . . things like that. But most of our patients are people like you, who have . . . who need—" she blushed and stumbled "—a rest."

Seeing that the nurse had embarrassed herself, I tried to brush over her comment. "You don't have to attend someone else?" I asked casually, settling down to eat.

"No." Amelia seemed relieved at the change of subject. "We have an adequate staff. I have only one other patient, and she's resting right now. Do you feel like talking?"

I nodded.

"Then let's move into the sitting room. It's far more comfortable." She carried my tray to a small table, and I sat down again and resumed my meal. "When you're through I'll comb your hair. It's so lovely! So many Spanish men marry women like you—with blond hair and blue eyes. And it's soft, not coarse like Mrs.—" She cut herself off, obviously remembering that she shouldn't speak of one patient to another.

"My daughter has hair just like mine." I stopped, aware that I had fit another piece into the puzzle. My daughter? But Amelia did not seem surprised. She knew more about me than I did myself.

"Yes, I know. You have her picture beside your bed." She rose and brought it to me.

I gazed at the photograph with a glow of pleasure. "Mimi . . . that's her name. She's just turned six." I found nothing threatening in the picture. Mimi stood beside me, her small hand in mine. She was dressed in play shorts and halter, and her hair hung loosely over her shoulders. I turned my attention to my own image. "Is this the way I had my hair when I came in here?"

"Yes, madam. I'll comb it that way now, if you'd like."

I nodded. I was suddenly no longer hungry, for I had remembered that Lorenzo was the one who took the picture. Lorenzo! A shadow that chilled my heart.

Amelia was gentle with the comb as she pulled out the few snarls that sleep had put in my hair. She brushed it next, using long, firm strokes that felt good against my scalp. Then at last she gathered it all on my right side and combed the end into a long, fat curl. "You look so . . . distinguished!" She stepped back to admire her handiwork. "Are you comfortable in that chair?" She took my tray and placed it on another table, out of my way. "Herb tea?"

I nodded. From a drawer she produced two cups and poured some tea for us both. Then she sat opposite me again. "Do you want to talk?"

"Oh, yes!" I felt suddenly close to her, as if she had

been my friend for a long time. "The doctor said I've been here almost a month. Did I seem depressed when I arrived?"

"Oh, yes, madam. And very exhausted. But that's the way most of our patients are."

A sudden fear gripped me. "Do most of your patients . . . like me . . . stay very long?"

Amelia seemed to hesitate before she answered. "Some of our patients get well very quickly. But . . . ." She didn't continue, for she had seen my expression.

I knew I had not been able to hide my alarm. Some of her patients got well quickly. But others remained for the rest of their lives! "Tell me—" I struggled to keep my voice calm "—did my husband bring me here?"

"Why, of course. He was very worried about you; you seemed so distraught. He signed all the necessary papers. But that's what usually happens. Some men don't seem to realize how skilled Dr. Shabib is. They're surprised when they are able to take their wives home again—totally recovered."

The shadow was back once more. Lorenzo had put me in this hospital. And now I knew what kind it was. I was a mental patient! I would remain here until Lorenzo was sure it was safe for me to return home.

I knew now the fear that had troubled my dreams. Whose safety had to be assured—mine or his? If I remembered much more, would I be too great a threat to him?

"Please, I think I'd like to rest now."

"Do you want to go to bed?" Amelia's eyes reflected her concern.

"No, thank you. Open this drape, too, would you, please? I think I'd like to look out for a while."

She did as I asked, and then walked to the door. "I'll drop back before Mr. Santos comes to visit, if he gives us any warning. One reason for your being here on the first floor is that he can come and go without paying attention to regular visiting hours. His business, you know." She smiled reassuringly. "I'll put another Valium near your bed. Just in case you need it."

When she was gone I sat staring out at the park. It was starting to drizzle now, spattering the window. Would I ever again feel the fresh air against my cheeks? Somehow I had to decide just how I should act to convince Lorenzo he could trust me once more. If I failed . . . .

I shuddered. Even the beauty of the room in which I sat could not compensate for the loss of my freedom.

Chapter 2

The rain began in earnest just as Amelia arrived with my dinner. She placed the tray before me and glanced toward the darkened window. "Shall I close the curtain, madam? Rain can be depressing."

"No, thank you. I wish I were out there. I've always loved to walk in the rain."

"Not this rain, I'm afraid. It's cold, and the sidewalks are slippery. You can be thankful you're safe inside."

She bustled about the hospital room, smoothing the sheets, preparing for my sleep. But I had no wish to go back to bed. I had dozed for part of the afternoon and now I felt refreshed—and hungry once more.

And fearful. "Did you say that Mr.—my husband was coming to visit me tonight?"

"He has come every day, madam. But he usually arrives late. I don't think you should wait up for him; you've already strained yourself by staying up so long. If you want, I'll come in and wake you as soon as he arrives. Do you feel like sleeping?"

"I don't know. Not at the moment, anyway. Can you stay again?" I asked. Suddenly I wanted some company.

She dropped into a chair, facing me. "For a little while. My other patient is restless." She gestured toward the rain-streaked window. "You really like weather like this?"

"Sometimes. It's been a long time since I've seen a rain just like this one. Our rains are usually much softer, and a lot warmer." I stopped. I had answered so easily. I seemed to recall a warm climate, with much bright sunshine and lush green tropical plants. But where was that? In my home? "Amelia, I hope you don't think I'm being silly. Where is this place?"

"Oh!" She seemed concerned that she hadn't told me before. "In Paris, of course."

Paris. I was in a clinic in Paris. How had I got here? There was so much I didn't know. Depression suddenly came over me, and I had no wish for further conversation. Nor for food. I pushed the plate away, and Amelia rose immediately.

"All done? Shall I bring in some hot chocolate later?"

I shook my head. "No, thanks. If you don't mind, I'll sit up a bit longer. I can make it to bed without help."

She smiled. "Fine. I'm glad you're feeling so much better. I've left a Valium there on the table beside your bed, in case you have trouble dropping off. Sleep tight, and I'll see you in the morning. The night nurse will be around if you need anything."

"Thank you. You're very kind," I told her.

She nodded, smiled once more in my direction and whispered her way out of my suite. I turned again to my study of the night scene.

There was precious little to see. Darkness . . . broken by one dim streetlamp and the square of light that spilled from my window. The park was invisible. I stared into the blackness without attempting to pick out any details, my thoughts once more turning inward. I would sleep better if I unraveled a few more threads in my private mystery.

Besides, the image of Lorenzo Santos had returned.
A tall man, with broad shoulders and narrow hips,
and the sharp, penetrating eyes of a bullfighter. Yet
he was no matador; he was . . . a dealer in fine art
pieces! The feeling of triumph returned. I was getting
somewhere again. I could visualize his wide mouth,
turned up in a patronizing smile as he looked at me.
He was handsome—and distinguished. The kind of
man who would want a regal-looking wife. And a
woman younger than himself. Was he the father of
my lovely, blond Mimi?

No answer came to that question, though the
uneasiness returned. To rid myself of it, I rose and
continued my exploration of my suite. I found a large
walk-in closet containing a number of expensive
dresses. Mine, of course. I also located my purse, and
rifled through it eagerly. In it was an answer to one
earlier puzzle. A small card in a pouch on the front
of the purse carried a message: "In case of accident,
contact Señor Lorenzo Santos, 17 Calle San Feliz,
Palma de Majorca, Baleares, Spain."

"In case of accident . . . ." Memory came back to
me in ragged bits and pieces. There had been no
accident, but nevertheless this card had helped me
on that terrible day when I suddenly discovered I
could no longer move at all. I had been found sitting
on a bench not far from the cathedral of Palma, in a
lovely square where I often walked while my husband
was at work. I sat immobile, my eyes staring ahead
without seeing, incapable of responding when the
policeman on duty spoke to me.

He had taken me to the station, searched my purse
and found the card. Miguel had picked me up that
afternoon in my husband's white Mercedes.

Miguel . . . another piece in the jigsaw puzzle. Lorenzo's chauffeur. His right arm, Lorenzo had once
called him. Yet when I recalled the swarthy face with
the low, sloping forehead, and the big, muscular body

of the man, I knew that he had always been an enigma
to me. Helpful to Lorenzo, kind to little Mimi, yet at
the same time frightening—like a wild ape kept on
a chain.

Lorenzo was away so often, on business. But what
was his business? An art dealer. I had found that
answer already. But then why was I still unsatisfied?
Why did I feel uneasy at his many absences? The fear
returned, and I pushed the thoughts back. I did not
wish to force myself to recall too quickly. The doctor
had warned me to be careful.

Seeking a distraction, I rose and turned off all the
lights in my room. Immediately the rain-swept street
outside became more visible, and I leaned forward
in my chair. Lorenzo would be along soon, and I felt
a need to see him approach—to be prepared before
he entered the room. This man—my husband—was
as yet an unknown quantity to me.

Night obscured much of the park, except for those
circles of pale brightness beneath the street lamps.
The naked branches of the trees were shining wetly
again in the reflected glow. The street was empty of
cars, and no pedestrian could be seen struggling against
the blowing force of the storm.

I found myself shivering as I stared out into the
darkness that suddenly seemed sinister as well as
mysterious. Then I rose abruptly. I could not permit
myself to think such thoughts. My confusion must
not overwhelm me as I searched for what I knew and
yet did not know.

Without turning on my light, I rose and stepped
back into my hospital room. I glanced at the pill Amelia
had left on the bedside table, but I had no intention
of taking it—at least not yet.

Timidly I pushed open the door to the corridor. It
was not white and sterile, as I had expected it to be,
but instead resembled the reception hall in a fashionable home, with a stained-glass door at one end.

In the light that came from beyond it, I could see the pattern of a daffodil formed in the colored glass.

I moved silently toward that door and peered through the colored panes. Beyond was a more typical hospital scene. A neatly garbed receptionist sat at a large stationary desk. The room itself was oval shaped, with elegant couches and chairs distributed tastefully about. The woman at the desk was not aware of my presence. As I watched, she rose and disappeared through a door much like mine, on the opposite side of the room. Its glass was formed in the shape of an iris.

I felt surrounded by a blanket of silence and knew an intense urge to hear another voice—before my mind began again to play tricks on me. My room, when I stepped back into it, seemed oppressively warm, as if it were closing in on me, and I longed to be out in the cool rain. I realized, finally, why I waited so eagerly for Lorenzo's appearance. I had had enough of isolation. If I was to regain my memories, I preferred to do so in my own home—among friends. With my daughter nearby.

Had I been given a choice when I was brought to the hospital? I felt sure I had not. Nor did I dare to ask about the details of my arrival. Not when Lorenzo arrived. Not with the night nurse. I would wait, I decided, until Amelia was again on duty. She, at least, was friendly.

Yet why was I afraid to ask for details from Lorenzo? Of all people, my husband should be most sympathetic . . . shouldn't he?

I resumed my chair and struggled again with my memories, examining the facts I had so far assembled. I was a most envied woman in Palma. A handsome husband, all the money I could ever need. Two lovely homes, one within the city, the other close to the ocean, on the far side of the island. We had once been described as the most attractive couple in all of Majorca.

Again the feeling of foreboding returned, and I brushed the memories back. Too fast. I was forcing myself again. I had to be careful or I would slow down my recovery.

I saw the window itself clearly for the first time, and realized that a portion of it could be opened. An upper section, too high for a patient to crawl through. I climbed on a chair and pushed it open. The cool air hit my face and I gasped in delight. As the drops of water touched my cheeks I remembered how, in Connecticut, elderly ladies sat pressed against the windows, watching the children at play on the beach. Was I like them—a participant no longer? My smile faded and depression closed in once more.

Yet it did not remain. Instead, the memory of my childhood flooded back. I had grown up on the silver sands and the windswept beaches near Old Saybrook, Connecticut. When I closed my eyes, I could see the old church tower, half-hidden behind the rolling hills of sand, the slim pine trees, pointing upward, like arrows aimed at heaven. The sea gulls circling overhead. The tufts of grass that grew . . . .

My dream! I had been dreaming I was a child again. But then what was the dark shadow that filled me with such fear? A sharp pain cut across my temple.

Suppressing a feeling of panic, I turned my attention once more to the street. I could see a figure crossing the park, appearing in the halo of each lamp it passed by. A woman, that I felt sure, for it was a small form, and the cape that covered it was feminine in design. A hood covered the woman's head, protecting her from the blowing rain.

Just as the figure reached the street near the one lamp that was not lighted, a car came racing toward the hospital. The curtain of rain dimmed its headlights. I felt sure Miguel was driving, though I could not determine the size or make of the vehicle. He had a style of his own. Impatient, as if caution were foolishness. Any other driver would move slowly in such a storm. One more piece in the puzzle!

If that was Miguel, as I supposed, then Lorenzo would soon arrive. I rose and reached for the light switch.

I never touched the button. The scene outside my window changed in that instant to one of tragedy. The hooded woman had stepped out onto the street and I heard the thump of impact as the car hit her with one corner of its bumper. The vehicle swerved to avoid running over the crumpled form, glanced against the lamp post and skidded to a stop on the sidewalk. For what seemed like an eternity, nothing moved.

I clutched at my throat, holding back my cry of alarm. Was Lorenzo hurt? Dead? And the woman . . . ?

I exhaled with relief when two men climbed from the car. I could see it clearly now, and I knew my assumption had been right: the car was Lorenzo's white Mercedes. And the man who leaned over the still form on the road was my husband.

He stood up and gestured to Miguel, who immediately ran toward the clinic. He seemed to glance up at my window as he passed, and I drew back in alarm. Had they seen me watching?

Moments later Miguel reappeared with two white-coated orderlies, who carefully placed the injured woman on a stretcher and carried her back into the building. Lorenzo walked purposefully alongside them, the grim set of his jaw highlighted in the moonlight.

I hurried quickly to the hallway. Lorenzo was already inside the reception area, and he was gesturing wildly as he spoke. I had intended to rush out to help, but something caused me to draw back. I pressed myself against the wall, in the shadow, and listened.

"Miss Angele!" Lorenzo seemed to know the receptionist very well. "You must call the doctor."

As the woman reached for the phone, Lorenzo

brushed her arm away. "Please, miss. I do not wish to cause you any problem, but do not call the police." He reached over and pressed the intercom. "Just get Dr. Shabib."

"I'm sorry, he isn't here." She sounded upset.

"Then, dammit, get the doctor in charge! I know you aren't alone here!"

She spoke softly into the intercom, and almost immediately an authoritative-looking man stepped into the reception room. "Yes, Miss Angele?" He saw the injured woman and hurried to her side. After briefly examining her, he turned to Lorenzo, his voice troubled.

"This woman's leg is broken. She is likely badly bruised and appears to be suffering from concussion. It's difficult to determine the full extent of her injuries right now, but I suggest you take her at once to a hospital."

"This is a hospital." Lorenzo was fuming. "You surely don't intend to send her away!"

"Mr. Santos, we are a very specialized and, need I remind you, very expensive clinic. Who will pay for her care? Are we to give her a room out of charity? Please, Miss Angele, call the state facility and notify the police."

"No!" Lorenzo stepped again to the telephone and pressed his hand on the receiver so Miss Angele could not pick it up. "Do you not see? This is a matter of honor! I was the cause of her accident; the least I can do is pay for her treatment. And I choose to have her treated here, so I can see that she is treated properly!"

He frowned at Miss Angele. "As for the police, surely you can see what a report of such an accident could do to my driving record. I must travel by car in my business—and I need a chauffeur, since I do much of my paperwork while on the road. Of what use is a police report—to assure that the victim is cared for? Well, I shall guarantee that—without any police! Here!" He fumbled in his pocket and removed a checkbook. "I'll pay for the preliminary examination and her first week of treatment in advance. And if you don't accept the word of Lorenzo Santos, you can check my credit with Dr. Shabib."

"No, wait," the doctor interrupted him, waving away the proffered check, "your word is fine. It's all right—the patient may stay here; we will look after her. I recognize that you are a good friend of Dr. Shabib, and because of your association with him I feel I can safely do as you ask."

He then turned to the orderlies and instructed them to take the unconscious woman to the clinic's emergency room, where she would be examined thoroughly and treated for her injuries. Within minutes she had been lifted onto a white-draped, narrow, wheeled table and escorted through a set of double swing doors. In the brief glimpse I caught of her I noted that she was young, and evidently poor, for her clothing was cheap and she carried a plastic handbag.

Lorenzo was facing me, and I could see how greatly he was relieved. "Thank you, doctor. I assure you, I will remember your consideration. I feel very responsible for the girl and I just couldn't see myself allowing her to go to one of those overcrowded public hospitals when I can afford to give her the best of care. I will tell Dr. Shabib how grateful I am."

Turning then to the receptionist, he pressed some bills into her hand. "This is for you, Miss Angele, as compensation for all the trouble I have caused you. I trust you will understand when I say I would prefer that Mrs. Santos not know of this unfortunate accident. It would only upset her."

The doctor raised his eyebrows slightly when Lorenzo offered the tip—obviously a large one, from Miss Angele's expression—but he merely nodded. "Yes, it's a good idea not to tell your wife. She is recovering well, and we don't want to set her back. Do you still wish to see her?" he asked Lorenzo. "I can see if she is awake."

Lorenzo shook his head. "No, thank you. As you say, she's probably sleeping. I'll see her in the morning, when I come in to speak with Dr. Shabib."

"If that's your wish." The doctor was all business. "The young lady will be in the iris suite, across from your wife's accommodations. It will simplify your visiting them both." He paused for a moment, rubbing his hands together. "Now, if you will excuse me, I must attend to the patient." He was gone without waiting for Lorenzo's reply.

Lorenzo, too, seemed satisfied that the problem was over. He gestured to Miguel, said his goodbyes to Miss Angele and vanished from my sight, presumably on his way back to the car. He had not once even glanced in the direction of my room.

I crept silently back to my window and watched as he returned to the street. I felt mixed reactions to the entire affair. Obviously the accident had not been his fault. Why, then, was he so concerned for the victim? Was she someone he knew? A mistress, perhaps, whom he had planned to meet as soon as he left me? If so, why had she stepped out in front of the car?

I knew I was letting my imagination run wild, but I could not contain it. Why was Lorenzo so opposed to calling the police? And why had he decided not to visit me after all? Did he dislike seeing me? Did he wish I were the one lying injured? I felt the headache returning and forced myself to abandon my search for answers. Maybe tomorrow they would come, when Lorenzo came back.

Out on the wet, dark street, Lorenzo and Miguel stood examining the damaged Mercedes. They pushed against the bent bumper, but it did not straighten. Miguel circled the car, evidently checking for damage to the tires. When he returned to Lorenzo's side, he

seemed pleased. Yet Lorenzo was not placated.
Through the open window I could just make out his
angry tones. "Why tonight, dammit? Any other time
and it would have been so simple. Stupid female! So
you think you can repair it?"

Miguel nodded. For the first time that night I saw
Lorenzo relax. "Well, then, let's see if we can get it
to start."

It took a few minutes, but finally the Mercedes
roared back to life. I followed it out of sight down the
street. Lorenzo had been fortunate. His secret, for
whatever reason he wished to keep it such, was safe.

Except that I had been a witness. Lorenzo had not
once looked toward my room, not even as he climbed
back into his car. Yet if he cared so little for me, why
had he visited me every day during my illness? And
would I see him more often now that his youthful
victim shared the same hospital?

I hurried to my bed and turned on the reading
lamp. The Valium was waiting where the nurse had
left it, and I took it hoping it would soothe me into
sleep. As I felt the drowsiness come, I thought of the
girl who lay in the room opposite mine. I would have
to see her to get answers to my worries. She had
seemed too young to be having an affair with
Lorenzo. . . .

Then I remembered her dress, and I smiled. My
suspicions must be wrong: Lorenzo would never allow a mistress of his to dress so poorly. He even
helped choose the dresses his clerk, Dolores, wore
in the art gallery.

The realization that my jealousy must be un-
founded gave me a new feeling of satisfaction. I had
been wrong. Was I wrong, also, in my fear of my
husband? Were both of these reactions only the result
of my breakdown?

I'll visit her tomorrow—after Miguel is gone. The thought
comforted me. She would be lonesome and confused.

I could help her—and maybe, as I spoke to her, I could help myself, as well.

Suddenly I knew I would not see Lorenzo the next day. I'd pretend to be asleep, if necessary, when he arrived. Somehow, I didn't trust him, and I had no wish to listen to whatever lies he might have prepared. Nor did I wish to put to a test my fear that he planned to keep me confined for the rest of my life. Not yet, anyway. First, I had to remember everything—especially the cause of my mental breakdown. I wanted no more surprises.

Chapter 3

"Good morning!" Amelia approached my bed. "I tried to wake you earlier, when your husband was here, but you slept too soundly." She fussed with my covers. "He stayed as long as he could, but he had to leave for a business appointment. He gave me this note for you." And she pulled a paper from her pocket.

I read it as she bustled from the room. It was very brief, and almost impersonal: "Crystal, I'm off for about eight days. Business. Lorenzo."

No "I'm sorry you were asleep." No "Love, your darling husband." Nothing to show that he cared for me at all. Yet he was paying for my stay in this expensive hospital. Was his concern for me based on a wish to keep me under his control? If so, what had made him feel I needed to be confined in a clinic?

I wanted desperately to ask about the girl who had been brought in by Miguel and Lorenzo, but I decided to wait until a more appropriate moment—or until Amelia mentioned her. But as a result of my preoccupation with the stranger, I felt in no mood for conversation. When Amelia had combed and brushed my hair, and had brought me a new robe from my closet, she departed with the promise to be back around two with a light snack to tide me over until dinner.

Once more I was free to watch the street outside my window, and to struggle—when I had the strength—with my memories.

By two, when Amelia returned, I was lonesome, and she stayed with me for a few hours. This time I seemed able to break down some of her reserve. She informed me that patients came to this clinic from everywhere. Dr. Shabib helped movie personalities, politicians, writers—and all, when the cure was over, returned to normal lives. Her loquaciousness encouraged me to ask the question most important to me at the moment.

"Amelia, are there any new patients here for treatment other than for a nervous breakdown? You know, regular medical problems?" I watched her closely as I spoke.

"No-o. . . . " There was a hesitancy in her voice. "Not that I know of, madam. . . ."

I let the matter rest there. But in the days that followed I grew impatient with the pretense. At last, on the third day, I decided to end the little game. It was possible, I knew, that the girl had been transferred to another hospital. Yet the doctor had assured Lorenzo that the clinic was prepared to care for her after all, and somehow I felt she was recuperating there.

When I heard Amelia approaching my room, I turned to the phone that sat on my bedside table. I had wondered at its value, since I received no calls, but now an idea had come to me. Lifting the receiver, I immediately began speaking into it, certain the nurse would hear me. "Yes, Lorenzo, I'll find out how she is. Just don't worry; I'm sure she's all right." I paused, as if listening, then continued, "I love you, too, darling. Come back soon. I'm sorry I was asleep when you were here." I made a kissing sound and then dreamily hung up.

Amelia was standing near the foot of the bed, beaming. "I'm glad Mr. Santos called."

"So am I. He must have been in a hurry when he left." I lifted the cover on my tray and casually picked up my glass of juice. "Oh, by the way, he asked about the girl he brought in—the one that was injured when she stepped in front of his car. I told him I'd let him know."

Amelia smiled. "Oh, she's fine! I didn't think he wanted you to be bothered, or I'd have mentioned her before."

"Don't worry about it. I understand. Then she wasn't seriously injured?"

"No, not at all. We were all very pleased. Her leg is in a cast, but the break wasn't too bad and should heal very quickly. She has a few bruises, but otherwise she got off quite lucky." She paused, as if considering whether to continue. "She does have a problem, though. Do you know her well?"

"Not at all. She's a stranger to both me and my husband."

"Oh, yes." Did she believe me? For that matter, was I telling the truth? Was I sure Lorenzo did not know her?

The nurse continued, "She isn't wealthy at all. In fact, she's quite worried because she lives alone. I think she's worried about her job." Amelia poured a second cup of tea for me. "I haven't pried, but I think she cries when she's alone."

"Oh!" I felt overcome with guilt, as if I were to blame for her troubles. "Has she had any visitors?"

"One, yesterday. An older man, carrying a briefcase. I think he was her lawyer—or something like that. But I don't think she's planning to sue." She said the last quickly.

"I don't think she'd have much of a case. She stepped out in front of the car. I saw the whole thing."

Amelia was understandably surprised to hear this, but my account of the episode I had witnessed that night was so matter-of-fact that her worry on my behalf was quickly allayed. We casually discussed the unfortunate patient further. Despite the suggestion that the girl might be planning a court case, I felt sorry for her. So alone—so worried about her future. And to be handicapped by a cast!

"Amelia, is there a flower shop near here?" I inquired.

"Yes, just down the street."

"Good. I want you to send her a bouquet of roses. Have them put it on my bill. Oh, what's her name? I'm afraid my husband couldn't remember it."

"Valerie Roberts. She's an American, and quite a pretty girl, though a little thin, if you ask me." I wasn't surprised. Amelia was quite stout.

"What does she do most of the time?"

"Read. She was carrying a big book in a shopping bag. She draws a lot, too. I believe she's a dress designer." She continued confidentially, "I don't think she knows you're just across the hall."

"Is she still in the iris suite?" I asked.

"Yes. As I said, just opposite yours. You know you're in the daffodil suite, don't you?"

"Yes. I saw the lovely stained-glass door. It's a nice touch. There's something so cold and impersonal about rooms identified only by numbers."

Amelia smiled, obviously pleased at my compliment. When she left with my tray, I hurried to the closet. Should I dress before I made a visit? Or would Valerie be embarrassed if I seemed to be too wealthy? I decided, at last, that my robe was quite appropriate. After all, we were both patients in the hospital. Then I paused, uncertain again. We were not here for the same reasons. She might not appreciate a visit from a woman whose mental powers were—unbalanced.

If she asked me why I was here, would I be able to answer? Why had I been brought in? Oh, I recalled the feeling of helplessness that had come over me as I sat immobile on the bench, unable even to respond to the questions of the policeman who found me. But what had caused my sudden illness? I could not remember. I turned abruptly and hurried down the hall. If I did not visit her soon, I'd talk myself out of it entirely.

Valerie was lying in bed when I opened her door and stepped inside. She glanced up, and I realized she was somewhat older than I had imagined her to be. Twenty-two, maybe; possibly twenty-five. Her eyes were large and beautiful—green, with a fire in them that seemed to flare up when she saw me. Her skin was pale, partly from her confinement, but also naturally, and I wondered how long she dared stay out in the sun.

I felt a flash of recognition. I had seen eyes like that before. Then the sparkle was gone, and they turned dark, as if a shadow of indifference had closed off her thoughts.

I approached her bed. "I'm Crystal Santos. My husband was on his way to visit me when you were— when the accident occurred. I understand your name is Valerie."

She didn't seem at all surprised by my presence in the hospital—the nurses' gossip must have reached her. "Yes," she answered me, her smile wan. "If you're worried that I'll sue, forget it. I've been told I have no case at all." The smile grew suddenly, and she seemed to open up. "Not that I thought I did. But you know lawyers; they're out for whatever they can get. Actually, I feel quite guilty accepting all this help from you. It was as much my fault as your husband's—or rather, his chauffeur's. He was going too fast for a rainy night, I suspect—but I had no business stepping off the curb without looking." She gestured toward the flowers. "Amelia came running in with these a few minutes ago. They're from you?"

"Yes. I hope you aren't troubled by nightmares. An accident can be terribly traumatic."

"No, I'm fine." She gestured toward her cast. "Except for this leg. I'm afraid I wasn't thinking clearly that night. I had a letter to mail, and when I saw the mailbox I just headed toward it. Next thing, when I woke up here I was! I feel pretty lucky. A lot of drivers would have left me on the street. I gather there weren't any witnesses. Your husband would be justified in refusing any responsibility at all."

I nodded. I needn't tell her I had seen it all. She continued, "The least I could do in return for your husband's generosity was agree not to go to the police, as his lawyer requested. I certainly couldn't get better treatment—or more consideration. And all that would happen is that there'd be hard feelings. Did you see Mr. Anderson when he was in?"

I shook my head. "He never wastes time on purely social visits."

"Oh. Well, he told me Mr. Santos's chauffeur is quite an old man, who would suffer unnecessarily if there were an investigation. He assured me the man has been warned to drive slower from now on. I can't see any reason for making him suffer, when your husband has been so kind to me."

"Yes." I hoped I sounded convincing. "Of course!" She had loaded me with too much meaningless information. Who was Mr. Anderson? I could not remember hearing Lorenzo mention him. And as to describing Miguel as an aging servant too frail to endure an investigation—ridiculous!

I felt suddenly unsure of myself. "Well, I think I'll get back to my own room. No point in tiring ourselves. I'll drop by again, if that's all right."

Her smile was warm and her answer sincere. "I'd love it. I get awfully tired of being alone."

I felt convinced, as I crossed the lobby, that I had been wrong in suspecting Valerie of knowing Lorenzo before the accident. She was clearly an innocent victim of his impatience. But what was I? He seemed to be pushing me out of his life, as if he wished he did not have to deal with me. Had I done something to lose his confidence, to make him angry with me?

By the time I had reached my room I was again in control of my wild imaginings. How stupid I was! He was busy—and I was suffering from loneliness. He was my husband. I missed him, and I needed him. When he returned, everything would be all right.

Valerie and I visited for hours that afternoon—and in the days that followed. By the third day we felt like old friends. I arrived at her door right after breakfast. As usual, she called out for me to enter.

I found her sitting up in a chair. The robe she wore fitted poorly—obviously hospital issue. "Glad to see you up!" I greeted her. "You're looking a lot better."

"I feel better. I can't tell you what a drag it is to stay in bed for days at a time. Look!" She rose and hobbled around. "I can even walk! The doctor says I'll heal better if I keep moving." She led the way into her sitting room and pulled open a drawer. When she returned to my side, she held a sheet of paper in her hand. "Here. I drew this for you."

She offered me a sketch of an evening gown. I gasped in delight. This was not the drawing of an amateur. It was sketched on a high-style, long-necked mannequin with a hairstyle just like my own. The cut of the gown was simple and clean, with an elegance fit for a queen. "Why, Valerie, this is beautiful. Do you mind if I use it? I have a dressmaker back in Palma who could turn this into the gown of the season. It should be done in crepe, shouldn't it?"

She nodded, her face beaming with pleasure. "You

like it? Really? You're not just saying all that to make
me feel good?''

"Not at all. It's lovely. Are you a dress designer?
I mean, do you work at it professionally?''

"Oh, no! I wish I could. I've learned it isn't easy
to get a job in Paris, especially when you're an American.'' She looked depressed again. "I guess I'll just
have to call it quits and go back home.''

"You don't sound happy about the thought.'' I
cocked my head, studying her, then joked, "But you're
too old to have run away.''

She smiled at the picture I drew. "No, hardly. I did
come over here to make my fortune, though. I had
pretty high hopes. But I seem to have either too many
qualifications or too few. Most designers want to train
their workers themselves; they don't like people with
ideas of their own.''

"Of course not. You pose a threat. The day will
come when you might give them competition.'' I waited
for her to sit down opposite me. "Is that the only
reason you hate to go back?''

"Well, no. But it's the main reason. I'm not sure
how I'll get along with a leg in a cast. I've been working as a waitress to keep alive while I wait for my big
break. Now . . . .'' She paused. Her next words came
all at once. "Darn it! I just hate to go back and let her
say she told me so!''

"Her? A school friend?''

"No. My stepmother. If my dad were alone, as he
was before, I'd go back there to convalesce. But I can't
stand her. Maybe I'm just jealous—but I don't think
so. She's such a phony! And as soon as they were
married, dad began to talk about my leaving. I don't
think they wanted me around.''

"Your mother's dead, I suppose?''

"Oh, yes. She died years ago, and I've been taking
care of the house—and pop—ever since.''

I smiled. People can be so blind about their own

problem. "Did your dad know you wanted to be a dress designer?"

"Oh, sure. I've talked about it ever since I was a kid."

"Would you have come to Paris if he hadn't married?"

She didn't answer, but I could tell she was considering my words. I went on, "How long have you been gone?"

"About four years. I left as soon as I reached twenty-one. I took classes at first; I had an inheritance from my grandmother that paid the tuition. Then I began to look around for work. Honestly, it's hopeless! I've been told I'm overqualified, underqualified, have refreshing ideas but not enough structure, have plenty of good structure but poor ideas. . . . I'd be laughing now if it weren't so tragic. Darn it! I just don't want to admit defeat. Not yet."

She forced a smile. "Grandmother left me enough money to buy a car as well as pay the tuition, but I suppose I'll have to sell it now to pay the rent on my apartment and to keep me going until I'm able to walk again. I have enough saved for that."

"Then what will you do?"

"I'm not sure. That night—the night of the accident—I was going to mail a letter to apply for a job interview. I've got my bachelor's degree in general education, and I love working with children. I had hoped I could get a position with the Red Cross—or maybe with some other charitable organization, working with orphans in Africa. It isn't what I want to do the rest of my life, but it would give me time to sort things through, and perhaps I could save enough money to try here again."

"You don't have any friends here? What about a boyfriend back in the States? It might not be so bad going home to someone special."

She laughed. "Please, I'm not the kind to be swept

off my feet! Besides, it doesn't happen that way anymore. I just couldn't go along with all the games the
boys played when I was in college. And it might be
old-fashioned, but I tend to avoid a steady relationship until I feel there's more to it than just physical
attraction. I guess I'm pretty choosy. Part of it is that
I compare most fellows my age with dad, and they
just don't stand up to him."

"Maybe not. But that doesn't mean you should give
up looking. Marriage may not be very popular these
days, but it can be good."

I paused. Was I speaking from personal experience?
Was my marriage to Lorenzo a good one? I still felt
so in the dark about this man who was my husband.
Memory was gradually reconstructing the picture of
my life, but certain parts of the puzzle were missing.

I decided it was time to change the subject. "Then
you're alone in Paris? It doesn't sound as if you've
been having much fun."

"For sure I haven't! You know, I spent last Christmas with my landlady. She's all the things I hope I'll
never be—kind of grumpy, but really very pathetic.
There sure are a lot of lonely people in the world. Is
that why so many of them marry over and over again,
no matter how bad their marriages are? Just to avoid
being alone?"

"I suppose so. But you aren't actually alone—at
least, it doesn't sound as if you are. You could go
home."

"You wouldn't say that if you understood. No—I
mean it when I say they wanted me to leave. I suppose
they had a point. Most women my age are married,
or off on their own. Or at least they're well established
in their careers."

"So? You're not so old. And you certainly seem
determined enough. I'd probably have gone home at
Christmas if I'd been in your place."

"Well, I just can't. It really isn't the same. Helen

started out by redecorating the whole house. I felt as if she was trying to wipe away any memory of my mother. She even changed the paintings on the walls and the layout of the garden. New furniture . . . everything! And dad went along with her. It used to be such a pretty house—you know, a typical New England, Cape Cod type, with dormers and sloping roof. And a little picket fence enclosing the kitchen garden. Lots of tradition. It's been in my family for more generations than I can remember. She turned to her drawer and pulled out a picture from her wallet. "See."

I took the photograph and studied it. There was something familiar about the building. Very familiar. I handed it back to her. "Thanks, it's lovely. Where did you say you lived?"

"Oh, in a town you've never heard of. I grew up in Connecticut." I watched her questioningly. "Well, in a place called Old Saybrook." She laughed as she held out another picture. "Here's a shot of my dad and me, just before he got married again."

I felt myself tingle with excitement. Old Saybrook! What an unbelievable coincidence. And she had lived there all her life? Then I had to know her. Yet her name was not that familiar. "You lived close to Old Saybrook? In town?"

"Well, no, not really. I lived about six miles east, on the other side of the Connecticut River. But my cousin lived in the town, and for convenience I call it home when people ask me. We use that post office, too."

I looked more closely at the picture of her father. "Do you have any other pictures? Of your cousin, maybe?"

She dug into the drawer. "I usually keep them in my purse, but it was rather badly mashed. I saved the wallet—fortunately. I'd have trouble getting copies of most of these pictures."

What I saw spread before me was a photographic record of my own past. The beach, the clumps of grass, the white houses and the picket fences. The green roofs. The boats resting on the shore, their sails tied close to the masts, rudders digging into the wet sand like sharks' fins.

And the children! The names I had forgotten, but those faces still lived in my memories. The boy from down the beach who used to pull my hair in school. The red-haired girl whose beauty I'd envied when I was in tenth grade. The first boy I'd had a crush on, when I was eleven.

One face stood out from the others. This was a boy I had known better than the others. I had spent days, when I was home on vacation from college, visiting with him, discussing our dreams. Then I had gone to join my father in Rome. I pointed at the familiar face. "Is this your cousin?"

"How did you know? Yes. His name is Mark—Mark Lefevre."

I remembered it all so clearly. Mark had been the closest thing to a boyfriend I had at the time. Not because I wasn't interesting to boys, but because I didn't feel at home with most of them. I'd spent much of my time as a kid in schools all over the world— until mother, deciding it wasn't good for me, had insisted on settling in Connecticut so I could get some consistency in my education. But by that time it didn't help: I already was too different. I spoke several languages, including French, Spanish and German. English felt no more like my native tongue than any of the others. I was accustomed to associating with important people, in exciting places, and the beaches of Connecticut seemed dull by contrast—at least much of the time. Only Mark seemed to understand me, and he never resented my knowledge. There had even been a period when we thought we were in love. It was then he had named his boat *Cris*. Everyone else thought it was just short for Criscraft, the builder. I was the only one who knew he had named it after me.

"I used to know Mark, when I was in high school, and in the first year of college."

"You did? Oh, how exciting! He was always my favorite cousin—we still keep in touch."

"Does he still live in Old Saybrook?"

"Oh, no. He left there years ago. Went to medical school in New York, and then took a position in Mexico City. If you knew him when you were in college, you must have known he was studying to be a doctor."

I remembered, of course, when she told me. I had gone off to Italy, to spend the summer, and then, when it was time to return to college, I had decided to attend school in Paris. Mother had joined dad as soon as I finished high school and started college, and she was obviously relieved when I chose to stay nearby. He had been stationed in Paris then, and it was fun to be a family once more. But then they had both died suddenly—in a train wreck.

I stared out the window. Was that what had caused my breakdown? I toyed with the thought for a time. No. It had happened too long ago. I felt no ache of loneliness when I thought of my parents. I had had time to grow accustomed to their being gone.

"Didn't Mark have a sister?"

"Sure . . . Mary. She married a Canadian and lives in Quebec. Their mother died a few years ago, and I guess you remember their dad died long ago."

I felt surprise that I was hesitant about asking the next question. "Is Mark . . . married, too?"

"Mark? Oh, no. I guess he's just crazy about travel and adventure. Or—" she lowered her voice "—perhaps he's pining for some long-lost sweetheart. Anyway, he's never married. Hey!" Her face brightened. "It wasn't you, was it? If you thought you were in love . . . ."

I laughed lightly. "No, I'm sure it wasn't me. Mark and I were good friends, but we really were just friends." Yet . . . were we, I asked myself. All I knew was that memories of Mark, and his familiar image in the picture I had just seen, brought back warm feelings to me now.

"Oh." Valerie seemed mildly disappointed at my response. "Well, I suppose it's just as well, since you're already married. But I keep trying. Mark would make a great husband!"

She began to gather up the pictures and stuff them back into her wallet. I watched her absentmindedly, aware for the first time of her resemblance to Mark. The same red hair and fair skin. The same strong jaw—except hers was feminine. The same green eyes. That was why she had seemed so familiar the first time I saw her. . . .

Suddenly my head was filled with my private pictures of the past. I had been eighteen, so certain of my sophistication, so proud of being a college student at last. He was twenty-two, already in premed and, despite his intelligence and scholastic achievements, still immature emotionally. We were more like two kids than young adults. It had been a short romance, filled with fun rather than passion. We had played at the idea of being in love—but we had both been too committed to our future plans to let ourselves explore such a relationship. We didn't even correspond after I left for Europe.

I was eager to know more about him. "Does Mark ever come abroad in his travels?"

"He keeps writing that he's planning a trip, but so far he hasn't made it. I guess he's more interested in visiting his sister in Canada." She pulled out a small address book. "Hey! Would you like her address? If you knew her . . . ."

"I'd love it." I hadn't been as close to Mary, but

we had liked each other—if for no other reason than my friendship with Mark.

She thumbed through the pages and began to write on a slip of paper. "Don't tell her about my trouble, will you? If she knows, it might get down to my dad."

"I'll have to mention that I met you. Otherwise, how would I get her address?" I smiled at Valerie's concern. "Don't worry, I won't give away your secret." I took the paper she held out. "It's really strange, finding out you're part of a family I knew when I was a child. We have a lot in common."

Valerie smiled. "I'm really glad I met you—even if I did have to be in an accident to do it! Just think, if I hadn't stepped off that curb, I'd have walked right past and we'd never have met at all. . . ."

I wondered at the coincidence of our meeting as I headed back to my room. It was strange—and fortunate. I knew I didn't want to lose contact with Valerie now that we had met. Yet I couldn't immediately think of any way to keep up our association once she was released from the hospital—and I returned to Majorca. Whenever that would be. . . .

The thought came suddenly. Maybe Valerie held the key that would release me from this fine, well-ordered prison. Already our daily talks had helped me to feel more secure in myself, more assured of my identity. Maybe, after seeing the improvement I had made, Lorenzo would take me out when he next came to visit.

Chapter 4

The next two days passed swiftly. Valerie visited me in my room, though she had to strain to cover the distance on her crutches. We spent hours remembering Connecticut, sharing the fun we had enjoyed at fish fries and clambakes. I tried to remember her then, but I couldn't. I had been four years older—too important to pay much attention to a "little kid" like her. But we had shared much, nevertheless.

She talked about Mark often, for he was her favorite cousin, as she had already informed me. He had attended medical school, and when he returned home for vacations he had entertained her with tales of his fellow classmates. I remembered that he had a marvelous sense of humor—an ability to laugh at his own discomfort as easily as at others'. Valerie's stories proved that his ability to make light of the most serious problems had never left him.

"You should have seen him when he took his finals in premed!" She laughed at the memory. "He was sure he'd failed. So when he came home, he announced that he'd decided to be a pirate instead of a doctor. He had us all worried stiff. Dad even tried to talk him out of it, and I thought he'd cut out before the exams were over. I was really sick about it. And then his results came in the mail. Wow—you should have seen him! He swam across the river and ran all the way to my house to tell me. You know, I thought he was just kidding, but he really had thought he didn't make it." She shrugged. "He's too smart to flunk. But he never was stuck-up about it."

I recalled that delightful modesty that had been so much a part of him. Yes, it would be like him to be afraid he'd failed a test when he'd actually passed at the head of the class—with honors! I had loved that reserve he had. I had always felt at ease with him—even when I talked about my dream of becoming an important diplomat, like my father.

I felt a wave of embarrassment. Maybe it would be just as well if Mark never visited Europe. He had achieved his dream, while I had failed completely at mine.

Valerie appeared that afternoon as I was reading. She paused at my door. "May I come in?"

"Of course. You're doing quite well on your crutches."

"Thanks." She held up an envelope. "I wrote another letter—asking for that job interview. I wonder if you'd mind taking a look at it. Maybe you can suggest something I've missed that would give me a better chance at being accepted."

I took the letter and read it through. It was well written, carefully phrased. If I were an employer, I'd jump at the chance to have someone who used the language so well. "I can see you know French. How many other languages did you say you speak?"

She smiled. "Five. English, of course, plus German, Italian, Spanish and Swedish. Languages have always been easy for me."

I sat quietly for a time, staring at the letter. I knew that if she sent the letter, she would almost certainly get some kind of work. But would she have time to

continue the pursuit of her chosen career? I doubted
it. Most charitable organizations were understaffed.
She'd be too busy with other people's problems to
devote herself to her own interests.

I tapped the pages lightly with my fingers. "A great
letter. I'm sure it ought to work. But before you send
it, I'd like to make you a proposition." I went to my
bedside and picked up the photograph of my daughter. "Here's a picture of Mimi, my daughter. She's
already showing an aptitude for languages. She speaks
English, Spanish and the Majorcan dialect." I realized
I was anxious to present a good case. I wanted Valerie
to agree to my request for my own sake as well as
Mimi's. "Would you be willing to come with me to
Majorca and teach her the languages you know? It's
time she had some steady schooling, and there are
no good private schools on the island. Everyone has
tutors—or governesses."

I spoke quickly now, afraid she'd say no before I
had a chance to present my entire case. "You'd live
at Soledad. You wouldn't have to act as a nursemaid;
Mimi already has a nurse. I'd be around most of the
time, so you'd have some adult company, too, besides
the servants. I'd be so very pleased if you'd at least
consider it."

She was staring at me with her eyes wide. "You
aren't just making this job up because you feel sorry
for me, are you?"

"Certainly not. I'd never be able to convince Lorenzo to accept you if you weren't qualified."

"You've spoken to Mr. Santos already?"

"No." I wished I did not have to make such an
admission. There had been no communication from
Lorenzo of any kind since he'd left Paris more than
a week before. "Not yet. But I'm sure he'll have no
objection. She's my daughter, not his. What I do for
her education is my business." I felt a mild amaze-
ment at the conviction in my own voice as I said this.

"Mr. Santos and I have no children. Mimi's father died in a plane crash, only a few months after we were married."

I realized my voice was cracked with emotion, and I hurried on in a more businesslike manner, trying to encourage Valerie. "You needn't be worried that there isn't room for you. Soledad has twenty-two rooms. You'll have a suite of your own. You won't have to concern yourself with Mimi at night. Simone has a room next to hers, so she can care for her then."

Valerie flushed. "Please, I wasn't thinking of that at all! I'm just afraid Mr. Santos might be annoyed. He might feel I'm taking advantage of what was, after all, an accident. I really don't feel that either of you owes me anything that hasn't already been paid many times over." She smiled sympathetically. "I'm sorry you had to bring that up. It must have been terrible to be alone at a time like that."

I touched her arm lightly. "Don't feel sorry for me. I've gone through that loss a long time ago. Yes, it wasn't easy. But I wasn't penniless, so survival was easier than it might have been. And now, as the saying goes, time heals all wounds." I held the letter out to her. "Well? What do you say?"

She took it absentmindedly. Then with sudden firmness she tore it up and tossed it into the wastebasket. "Thanks. If you haven't already regretted the offer, I'll take you up on it. Yes, I'd like to go with you to Majorca." She glanced ruefully at her cast. "Will you be leaving soon? I might be a burden to you if I'm still dragging this around."

"Don't worry. You'll have plenty of time for your leg to heal, either here or when we get home." I rose and took her hands in mine. "Oh, Val, I'm so glad you agreed!"

Her smile was a bit self-conscious. "I'm glad, too. It just isn't easy to have one's luck change so suddenly. It'll take a bit of time to get used to it." She swung herself lightly to the door. "Thank you so very much!" She paused. "I'll be ready whenever you are. All I have to do is sell my car. I don't imagine I'll need it on the island."

Valerie moved awkwardly down the corridor, and then I heard her say something. The answer was made in a masculine voice. I rose and returned to my bed. Evidently, I decided, Dr. Shabib was coming to see me.

Valerie had left the door slightly ajar, and it was pushed open by a masculine hand. The face that appeared was not that of the doctor at all. "Lorenzo!" I rose from bed and ran to meet him. "Oh, Lorenzo. I'm so glad you're here!"

He did not embrace me even though I threw my arms around his neck. His face was grim. "Were you having a visitor?"

"Why, yes." I could not hide my surprise. "Did you expect me to remain alone, now that I'm better?"

He seemed slightly placated. "No, of course not. But I didn't expect to see that girl in here. Why did you single her out?"

For one crazy moment I thought of making up some wild story so as to avoid telling him the truth. But something in his face told me I dared not. "I saw the accident, Lorenzo—from my window. I felt sorry for her. She's all alone."

He considered my words, his face expressionless, then asked, "Well, is there any more you can think of that we ought to do to compensate her for her foolishness? If you saw it, you know the accident was her fault—not Miguel's."

"Yes, I know. She does, too. Please, Lorenzo, don't be annoyed with me. She holds no grudge. In fact, she's consented to come back with me to teach Mimi. Isn't that wonderful? You know what a time I've had finding anyone qualified."

"And *she* is?" He spoke sarcastically, as if the only way to judge her was by her appearance—her clothes.

"Yes." I recited the list of languages she could handle. "All she has to do is sell her car. I suspect she'll need the money to buy some clothes that are suited to the warm climate."

He had been listening absentmindedly, as if he had already agreed before he began to question me. Now he nodded. "Fine. That's settled." He seemed to shake the lethargy away. "Well, then, are you ready to come back?"

I felt a momentary confusion. He spoke as if my departure from the island had been my idea! Once more I reached up and kissed his cheek. "Oh, Lorenzo, I've been so lonesome for you. . . ."

He couldn't conceal his surprise. He pulled free of my arms and held me back so he could look into my eyes. "Is it true, Crystal? You were waiting for me to return?"

My perplexity increased, and I probed for some answers. "I don't understand, Lorenzo. Did something happen between us that I don't remember?"

He was smiling. A satisfied smile that gave him an odd, strangely evil appearance. Then he laughed aloud, and the impression of evil vanished. He was a boy, filled with the delight of living. "No, my darling, nothing at all. It's just that you were so sick. You don't remember anything of what happened just before you came here?"

I shook my head. Then I reached up again and this time his lips met mine. "Nothing. Nothing at all. But it doesn't matter now, does it?"

I looked up into his face. I wanted him to show the tenderness a woman should feel for her husband. I wanted to know if he loved me. But what I saw in his dark eyes was a glow of triumph.

Chapter 5

The following day I left the clinic with Lorenzo, "totally cured," according to Dr. Shabib. We had a long conference with Valerie that morning. She, too, was eager to leave the hospital, and the doctor released her when she agreed to return for at least one more examination before leaving Paris to join me at Soledad.

At first Lorenzo showed little interest in my decision to hire my new friend. But he seemed to become more intrigued with the idea as we talked. Valerie once more mentioned her car. "I'll have to sell it, of course. I expect it's still parked where I left it. Not that I'll get much for it. It needs new tires—and the brakes aren't too good, so I won't be losing much."

Lorenzo spoke directly to her for the first time. "Don't be in too much of a hurry to get rid of it. Cars are at a premium on the island. As for brakes and tires, they can be fixed." He seemed to expand. "Let me take care of it. As a sort of thank-you for the cooperation you've shown, let me buy you new tires and get the brakes fixed."

She might have seen the surprise in my face, for she hesitated before answering. Lorenzo seemed oddly agitated. "You're going to be way out in the country most of the time, *señorita*. I'm certain you'll find the car most useful." She still did not respond, so he continued, "It will be a big help to me, as well. I do not like to have Mrs. Santos driving alone, and Miguel usually has work to do for me. If you have your car . . . ." He shrugged. "You can see it will be a convenience."

I could not remain silent. "Really, Lorenzo, I do have a car of my own. Surely you haven't sold it while I was ill?"

He put a hand on my shoulder. "My dear, you forget you have been very sick. Until you are definitely cured, I don't want you dashing about on your own. And the young lady is used to her own car. Why ask her to learn to handle yours? Besides—" he turned toward Valerie with the most winning smile "—I'm sure Miss Roberts will like the freedom of having her own transportation, even after you're back on your own."

Valerie watched us in silence, and I wondered if she thought we might begin to quarrel. I smiled at her. "You're right, of course, Lorenzo. Whatever you say."

He seemed to dismiss me. Now he spoke directly to Val. "If you don't mind, just give me the ownership papers and the keys. I'll have Miguel take care of the entire thing. You can either come with us now or, if you need some time to finish your business, follow us later. I'll arrange for your train ticket and a credit at the dock to cover your passage. Will that be all right with you?"

"Oh, yes." Valerie was obviously overwhelmed by Lorenzo's generosity. "I never expected to get my car fixed, too! You're really much too kind."

"Not at all." He rose to signal that we ought to leave. "After all, you're going to solve a problem that's been troubling us for some time. It isn't easy to get good teachers these days."

"The car won't be too much of a problem? I mean, if it's too difficult for Miguel to take care of it . . . ." Valerie paused. "Well, thank you again. Since it's all right with you, I'll stay for a few days. I still have a week left on my rent, and that should give me enough time to settle things here. It's a relief not to have to concern myself with selling the car."

To stop her continued show of appreciation, I took Lorenzo's arm and headed for the door. "Goodbye, then. We'll expect a note from you before you arrive." I pulled out a paper on which I had written the phone number of the store in Palma. "You can call this number if you're ready too soon to contact us by mail. And thank you."

"Thank *you!*" She took the paper. I followed Lorenzo back to my room.

A few months before, I would have accepted all of Lorenzo's kindness at face value. But something had happened to destroy my trust. Something stood between us. Was it the same thing that had put me into this hospital? When Dr. Shabib insisted I was completely cured, did he mean that my memory was restored—or wiped clean? Somehow, I suspected the latter.

I had little reason to recall my momentary doubt during the days that followed. Lorenzo traveled alone with me, leaving Miguel to handle Valerie's car and tickets. He drove the Mercedes himself, and I sat beside him, feeling temporarily at ease. Was it Miguel who frightened me? I started, once, to ask Lorenzo, but something held me back. If I was wrong—if Miguel only did what Lorenzo told him to—then I would be showing that I was not as well as Dr. Shabib claimed I was. I could be returned to the hospital if it appeared I had not erased from my memory whatever it was that had upset me.

Eager as I was to see Mimi again, I remained in Palma with Lorenzo to adjust to my new freedom and enjoy the one week of privacy that came so unexpectedly. We dined out and took long walks together along the wharf. And for those seven days I felt secure—certain that whatever had troubled me was past. My husband was still an enigma to me; I could not get beyond his reserve. Yet the time we shared was pleasant and I was grateful for the quiet friendship he seemed to offer me.

The harmonious feeling continued into the eighth day, when on receipt of a phone call from Valerie we drove to the wharf to meet the ferry. Lorenzo lolled against a banister on the dock, gazing eagerly toward the sea. The ferry was late. I touched his arm. "Goodness, darling, you seem almost upset. I'm sure the boat is all right. Remember, the sea was quite heavy last night."

He assumed an air of indifference. "Yes, I know. Just a habit, I suppose. As a boy I used to love to watch ships arrive in the harbor."

I smiled encouragingly. Lorenzo seldom spoke of his childhood, and I welcomed the change. Never could I remember feeling any closer to him—not even during the days of our whirlwind courtship.

It seemed perfectly natural for me to remember those times clearly. He had appeared at Soledad one day and asked if the house were for sale. When I said no, he was quite disappointed. But he had not gone away. Instead, he remained until he convinced me that I should be his wife.

Those had been such idyllic days! I smiled up at Lorenzo. If only we could continue to remember their charm.

He met my eyes. "Why don't you rest over there—on those bales of hay. I don't think you should strain yourself."

I did as he suggested. Already the warmth between

us was fading. I wondered if he sensed it, too. Was it something I had said—or done? Or was it because Miguel was returning?

The hay smelled sweet, like the warm summer sun on a fresh field. I sat idly watching Lorenzo. Again, my feeling of discomfort was returning. And this time I decided to face the problem. Miguel.

I closed my eyes and brought his picture to my mind. He had always puzzled me. He appeared so ugly—and clumsy. Yet I had been told once, when Lorenzo and I were first together, that Miguel had been a toreador. I could not visualize him moving lightly aside to dodge the horns of an angry bull. He appeared more of a type to face the animal head-on—and strangle it to death!

I was fully aware that he liked me no more than I liked him. We had quickly settled on a sort of unarmed truce. He tolerated me, even helped me if necessary—but only because I was Lorenzo's wife. And he clearly did not approve of our union.

Lorenzo seemed oddly attached to Miguel, in the same way an ordinary man is attached to his dog. Miguel was like a dog! His devotion to Lorenzo was unquestioning. And he resented me, as any favorite animal would resent an intruder into his relationship with his master.

When we were first married—back when Lorenzo had been so warm and friendly to me—he had told me that Miguel came from his home village, a small place in the mountains near the city of Algeciras, in southern Spain. Lorenzo had explained that his ancestral château had been bombed during the Second World War. The Santos de Corpierro domain now existed only in the memory of Lorenzo and his few friends. We had never even attempted to visit my husband's birthplace.

I realized that Lorenzo never spoke of it anymore. He had remembered it long enough to satisfy my curiosity, and then he wiped it from his consciousness. I sensed that he actively sought to avoid thinking of his past.

"Crystal! Here comes the ferryboat."

Hearing Lorenzo call, I rose and returned to the dock. Lorenzo might be more interested in the mechanics of unloading Valerie's car, but I was concerned with greeting my friend. Already Lorenzo was withdrawing from me, as he had before my stay in the hospital. I looked forward to having Valerie help banish my loneliness.

Miguel was the first down the ramp. He barely acknowledged my presence. Instead, he hurried to Lorenzo and stood talking to him for some time, his eyes on the cargo net that would lower the car to the dock. There were five cars to be brought ashore, and Valerie's appeared to be last in line.

The passengers began to stream across the ramp, and I turned away from Lorenzo and Miguel to better see Valerie as soon as she appeared. So many people seemed to be disembarking. . . .

"Crystal!" She was standing on deck, waiting her turn on the ramp. I saw her wave and I moved closer. She looked frail and delicate in a cotton print dress and light wool cardigan. In the week's time she had graduated from a full cast and a crutch to a small, light cast and a cane, and seemed to be managing very well with them.

She began to talk before she was halfway down the ramp. "Oh, Crystal, how nice you are to meet me! I've been standing on deck for the last hour to make certain I wouldn't miss the entry into port. It's gorgeous! The bay is so large—and so very blue. I can't get over it all. Just think, if I hadn't been foolish enough to step off that curb, I wouldn't be here now. I'd probably be fighting mosquitoes in some godforsaken jungle, trying to teach naked children how to read. I feel so lucky!"

I took her overnight bag and waved to Miguel. He came at once and took it from me, and I watched while he placed it in the white Mercedes. When he returned I gestured to him once more. "Please, Miguel, will you see to it that Miss Roberts's other bags are loaded in her car? We'll be taking it to Soledad."

Miguel glanced toward Lorenzo. "I don't think—"

Lorenzo broke in, "Don't do that, Miguel. I want to be sure the repairmen did a good job on her brakes. We'll check the car out before we deliver it to her." He saw my startled expression and continued quickly, "Crystal, my dear, I'll feel safer if you let Miguel drive you out in the Mercedes. I'll follow as soon as I've had Valerie's car checked, and then I'll ride back to Palma with Miguel. As simple as that! And then you'll have Val's car with brakes you can trust."

Something in his voice warned me that he would brook no disagreement. I glanced at Valerie, afraid she might have found his behavior surprising. But she seemed only appreciative of his consideration. I faced him once more. "If you say so, Lorenzo. Shall we wait for the car to be unloaded?"

Valerie stepped forward. "Please! I'll feel better if I know it's ashore."

Lorenzo nodded and wandered off to where the fourth car was being released from the net. The wait would not be long.

Valerie turned to me. "Is there another Miguel? An older man?"

I shook my head, embarrassed. "No, I'm afraid the lawyer who spoke to you at the hospital was not altogether truthful. Miguel is, as you see, a strong man. I apologize for not telling you then, but . . . ."

"Don't worry about it, it doesn't matter. I'm just glad everything happened as it did." Val seemed to be watching the ramp, as if there were still one more person to arrive and join our group. I followed her eyes but recognized no one. Then I let the moment pass. Probably she had found some temporary companion during the crossing, and now she had missed the opportunity to say goodbye.

Still . . . the island was small. "Val? Are you looking for someone special?"

She blushed. "Well, not special—just sort of nice. A young man named Patrick, whom I met on shipboard. I hoped I'd get a chance to introduce him to you."

"Patrick?" I felt apprehensive. "What did he look like?"

"Well, he's a rather ordinary kind of fellow, I suppose. He's a painter, on his way here to paint some of the old buildings. We had quite a lot to talk about, especially since he's been here before and could tell me all the places worth seeing. He even described your country home. Soledad, isn't it? Are strangers allowed on the grounds? I mentioned you and Mr. Santos, but he didn't seem to know you." She was searching the dock with her eyes. "He was wearing blue jeans and a beige sweater. He's really kind of nice looking; tall, slender—maybe skinny. But he has a kind of flair about him. I assume he's an American, because he talks like one, but he acts a bit more French. Really, he's kind of a funny mixture. Intriguing."

"Did he tell you where he would be staying? In Palma?"

"He didn't really say. But he did mention something about phoning a friend when he arrived." She looked puzzled when she was unable to locate him in the crowd. "Crystal? Do you know him? Or, at least, have you seen him on the island before?"

"I know him well. But I suggest we not talk about him in Lorenzo's presence. I'll tell you why later." I stopped abruptly. Lorenzo was approaching.

"Well, Crystal, the car will be down in a moment. Are you about ready to go?"

I nodded and turned toward the Mercedes. At that moment, Valerie screamed. "The car! Look out!"

Suspended in midair, Val's car began to sway. Then it twirled slowly. The front end broke free from the net and tilted downward. Any moment, it could slip out and crash onto the dock. I watched in alarm—too startled to speak.

For a brief pause no one moved. Then Miguel sprang to action. As the car slid forward, he caught the front bumper with both hands and pushed with all of his strength. The weight of the vehicle almost threw him backward, but he held on, literally forcing the heavy car to remain in the tenuous grip of the cargo net. On shipboard, the crew worked feverishly to lower the weight before the net tore and dropped its cargo onto the dock.

When the wheels touched ground, I exhaled in relief. Around me, others did the same. It had been a frightening moment. Had the weight shifted differently, or had the men on board been too slow in lowering the net, we might have been helpless witnesses to Miguel's death.

Miguel stood for a split second, staring at the car. Then with a smile of satisfaction he turned toward Lorenzo. He said nothing; neither did Lorenzo show any outward appreciation of what his chauffeur had accomplished.

Valerie rushed to Miguel's side. "That was amazing! I was so frightened. I would never have forgiven myself if you had been injured trying to save my old car. It isn't worth anything. . . . "

Still Miguel was silent. Lorenzo rested his hand on the hood of the car. "Good job, Miguel. I'll take over from here."

Miguel nodded, as if suddenly released from a spell. He turned and headed toward the Mercedes. Lorenzo called sharply, "Miguel! Don't forget the *señorita's* bags!"

Possibly it was the release of tension that started
my reaction. I was not certain. I knew only that Lorenzo was treating this amazing feat as if it were nothing. I turned to him, my hands clenched. "How can
you act like that?" I felt sure my face was red, but I
didn't care; I was too full of fury. "He was almost
killed. I thought he was your friend!"

Lorenzo stared back at me. His face was expressionless. Then slowly his eyes grew dark and narrow,
and I knew he wanted me out of his way. Why, I
could not tell. He glared down at me coldly, but made
no move to respond to my attack. Then, with a gesture
that told me he did not even consider me worthy of
acknowledgment, he turned away. "Miguel! Give me
the keys."

Miguel had found Valerie's luggage, and he ran
with it down the plank. He put the bags down when
he reached Lorenzo, dug into his back trouser pocket
and produced the keys to Val's automobile. Then he
resumed his burdens.

I had watched him in silence. And I continued to
watch him as he loaded the bags in the Mercedes's
trunk. The sound of an engine starting brought me
around, but I was not quick enough. Valerie's car was
already moving away. Lorenzo, at the wheel, did not
even bother to wave goodbye.

Chapter 6

Valerie watched uneasily as Miguel loaded her cases into the trunk of the Mercedes. "Are you sure he's all right? He might have injured himself. . . ."

I shook my head. "If he has, he won't tell me—or you. But I don't think he did. He's a very powerful man." I wondered if I sounded afraid of him, but if I did, Valerie seemed not to notice. She allowed me to lead the way to the car, and settled beside me without again mentioning Miguel.

When we were moving, I had a sudden inspiration. I leaned forward and tapped Miguel's shoulder. "Drive around the town for a while, please. I'd like Miss Roberts to see Palma before we head for Soledad."

He nodded and turned the wheel. We were moving slowly up the Paseo Maritima, the beautiful palm-lined boulevard that sweeps along the curve of the bay. Valerie was captivated by the scene and she gazed around her in silence. Miguel turned onto a narrower street. I could see he was heading for the cathedral.

As we made the turn, Valerie began to speak in a low voice. "I've been thinking about Mimi, Crystal. I must confess I'm a little nervous. What if she doesn't like me? I'm not really experienced as a teacher. Will I be able to do what you expect me to do? She might resent being made to study."

I chuckled at the thought of Mimi resenting anyone. "Don't worry, she's not a spoiled child. And she's eager to learn. I suspect she's more like her father than me. He was the most happy person I've ever met."

We turned onto Borme, the second largest avenue in Palma, and I paused to point out some of the most notable sights. Then I continued. "Alan and I were married six weeks after our first meeting. Dad was stationed in France, and Alan flew in from Australia with some diplomatic corps."

I smiled at the memory. It had been a terribly exciting period of my life. Alan had swept me off my feet. For understandable reasons, my parents did not approve of him—but I didn't care. I ran off with him and we were married in a private ceremony. "He was the most vital person I've ever known—eager to try everything. Then he volunteered to fly some Italian dignitary to a meeting in Switzerland. Terrorists hated the man and—" I still found it difficult to say the rest "—the plane exploded in midair. A bomb attached to the tail assembly." I swallowed hard, but the lump remained in my throat. "He never even knew I was expecting a child. Actually, I didn't, either—until later."

I felt a great relief. I had told Valerie the whole story without breaking down. Smiling to ease the tension we had both felt as I described my tragic first marriage, I went on, "But it's over now. I thought life would never be good again—but I was wrong."

"Is it ever exactly the same, though? Can one ever forget completely? Some sadness always remains."

"You're thinking of your mother, aren't you?" She nodded. "Well, to be honest, yes, you don't forget. But there comes a day when you can face the memories without hurting. You're at peace with the past. I suppose that's when you begin to recall the good things that happened—and you let go of the tragedy that ended it all." I looked up. "Oh, Val, you must look out! We're coming to the old section of Palma, where our town house is located. This is such a beautiful part of the city."

She smiled and glanced out. The street had narrowed, and it wound up the hill like a snake. I pointed toward the spire of the cathedral that lay above us. "It dominates the whole city, as it did when the kings ruled Majorca. I always feel as if I'm stepping into the past when I drive up this street."

She turned and met my eyes. Hers were sparkling with delight. "I'm glad you're happy now. You've earned the right to enjoy life again." She gestured around her. "All of this is compensation for all you've been through. Your husband—your lovely homes—this wonderful island."

I did not reply. Was my present life compensation for my past losses? I wasn't certain. Maybe it was my fate to remain on the outside—to approach happiness, but never to possess it for long.

Suddenly I wanted to put an end to the conversation. I tapped Miguel on the shoulder. "Park here, please." He slowed down and finally found a parking spot near the cathedral. I opened the car door and waited while Valerie followed. "This is the Seo, our famous cathedral. It's built entirely of rose-colored stone on the site of an old mosque. Once, you know, Majorca was mostly Muslim."

Valerie stared up at the imposing edifice. At the very top of the spire, the statue of the Virgin extended her arms as if to embrace the entire city. "It intimidates me." Val shuddered and looked away. "It looks more like a fortress than a church." She gestured toward the heavy pillars that supported the entryway, then turned and faced downhill. The city lay spread out before her like a child's toy model. The noon-hour lunch had begun, and the streets were crowded. I caught the fragrance of cooking meat and knew a small vendor's truck must be nearby.

I was about to lead the way back to the car when a movement near the cathedral caught my eye. A figure stepped from behind a pillar and waved. I gasped in surprise. Patrick! I turned to approach him, but he ran before I could move. I remembered my promise to tell Valerie about him. But was this the time to begin? I decided it was not. I'd wait until we were alone.

"Let's go, Val. Miguel's getting impatient." I took Valerie's arm and headed for the car. "We're just a little way from Casa Juarez, our city residence."

She showed no reluctance to depart. "How come it's the Casa Juarez, and not the Casa Santos?"

"Because Lorenzo's not a native of the island. He came from Spain about a year before I did, and he bought the place from the Juarez estate. And Majorca is a place of tradition. Names don't change just because of a new owner." I caught Miguel's eyes, and addressed him. "We'll walk to the house. You can take the car to the garage for the time being. I'd like to show Valerie the gallery, too, before we leave for Soledad."

Our house, like its neighbors, had a high, dark facade that gave a sinister appearance from the street. Yet as soon as we entered, the atmosphere changed. The front hallway was wide and high, with fine wood sculptures lining the walls. This had been a nobleman's residence, and it well suited its role as home of one of the rulers of the island.

As I led the way up the grand stone staircase, I realized that I was glad we were not going to stay on in the city. I did not really like this magnificent building. It felt cold. There was only one room in it where I felt comfortable.

I passed rather swiftly through the reception room, the "living" rooms where guests were entertained. It seemed to me so wasteful that this grand house was never filled with the sound of laughter—with the excitement of a party. Lorenzo was too individualistic a man to enjoy large gatherings. I had never seen him invite more than two or three guests at any one time.

When we reached the top of the staircase, I turned and looked down. Below was a smaller room, visible through a screen. It appeared cozy when viewed from a distance, yet I knew that the fireplace was too large, and the heavy, Spanish-style furniture was not really comfortable. I turned again and hurried on to the upstairs rooms.

I almost rushed Valerie through the other rooms. The master bedroom was impersonally formal in its furnishings, while the others were mostly unused. Except for my room: the one space where I had dared to leave my imprint.

Valerie gasped as she stepped inside. "Crystal! That picture. It's of the man I told you about—the one on the ferry!"

Despite my awareness that Miguel was down with the car and Lorenzo was not in the house, I glanced nervously over my shoulder. Then, with a self-conscious laugh, I told her brightly, "Yes, I know. He's my brother."

Delight was written on her face. "Your brother! Why didn't you tell me? Where is he?"

"Not here, I assure you. He and Lorenzo had a—a falling-out." My use of the old-fashioned term intimated that what had happened was of minor importance. "His name is Patrick Derbly. He lived with us here for quite a while last year, and did some work for Lorenzo. Then they had a disagreement, and Patrick left Majorca. Lorenzo mustn't know he's come back. Please, I can't explain any further right now, but it's important."

She smiled reassuringly. "If that's what you want, I'll never say a word. Thanks for telling me, though. It sort of explains why he acted so mysterious. And why he asked so many questions about you!" She chuckled. "I thought he might be your lover. He was so interested in everything I could tell him about you."

"We haven't corresponded since he left. First, I didn't understand that he wouldn't be coming back, and then . . . ." I did not continue. Then I had suffered my breakdown, and had been taken to the hospital.

I crossed the room and pulled back the heavy drapes that covered the windows. Valerie stared out in surprise. The house was built on a hill, and what was a third level inside was street level because of the slope of the land. I unlocked the door and stepped onto the balcony. A short flight of stairs led down to the narrow garden, which was shielded from the street by a stone wall.

I pointed to a small gate at one corner of the wall. "I sometimes come in this way, just to avoid going through all those empty, monstrous rooms. I feel good here."

"Do you stay in the city a great deal?" Val studied the streets that lay spread out below us.

"Not anymore. When we were first married, Lorenzo and I stayed here all the time. I didn't care then where I was, as long as I was with Lorenzo. But . . . ." I wondered if I ought to go on. Would it help Valerie to feel comfortable at Soledad and get along better with Lorenzo if she knew how things stood between us?

She remained silent, and that silence convinced me. She was not the type to pry, but she was clearly concerned. Like me, she would be caught in the strange intrigue that seemed to surround Lorenzo and his companions—unless she was properly warned. I did not look at her as I continued.

"It's just something that's hard to explain. He's an art dealer—I told you that, didn't I?" She nodded. "Well, he has a woman working for him. Dolores. She manages his gallery. She was his business partner long before I came into his life. I think she resents my presence. Maybe she even expected him to marry her. . . ."

Suddenly I didn't want to continue. Not right away, anyway. Lorenzo . . . the art gallery . . . Dolores. Images hammered at my brain, but the whole picture of what was troubling me would not yet take form. "I know!" I announced. "Let's go down to the gallery. You can meet Dolores yourself; she's really quite an extraordinary woman."

I moved without waiting for Val's response. As we reached the head of the stairs, I called to Miguel. He had the car ready as we entered the courtyard.

The gallery was located in the new section of Palma, and I realized again, as I did every time I approached the area, that I resented this stone and plastic copy of Miami Beach on so ancient an island. Yet here was the center of tourist life. The shops were filled with expensive items priced much higher than they would have been in Paris. There was an empty brittleness about this part of the city that spoke of money—and display.

The art gallery itself did some little bit to show a more dignified aspect of the tourist trade. It was luxuriously decorated in subtle colors, with fine pieces of furniture. The air conditioning assured both the comfort of the patrons and the preservation of the artwork they examined.

The entire appearance of the store was that of a fashionable home, with art pieces placed tastefully about. This was the most prestigious gallery in Palma— a must for the important travelers. Dolores, who operated the gallery alone, was perfectly suited to her position.

A Brazilian by birth, she spoke four languages fluently as well as the Majorcan dialect, which she needed to deal with the laborers who crated and uncrated the treasures she sold.

She was a striking woman in her mid-thirties, with a full, voluptuous figure and features typical of classic Spain. Her hair was jet black, with a natural curl that she kept under control by pulling it tightly back and rolling it into a large knot on her neck. She usually wore an attractive business suit, but I always felt she would have looked more appropriate in a costume like the one Carmen wears. With a rose over one ear.

I had known Dolores for three years, but she was still a mystery to me. She was unpredictable—exuberant one minute, depressed the next. At first I had tried to make her my friend, but without success. She refused to allow anyone to penetrate her reserve—except Lorenzo. With him she was at ease. It did not take me too long to realize that she tolerated me only because Lorenzo insisted.

She greeted Valerie politely and proceeded to accompany us through the entire gallery. She pointed out many individual pieces, even giving the history of some. She was the perfect hostess. Yet Valerie seemed eager to depart. I was almost relieved that she shared my reaction to Dolores, for I was uneasy throughout the entire tour.

I led the way from the gallery to a small café. When we were seated, I ordered two espressos. Then I turned to Valerie. "Well? What do you think of her?"

"I'm impressed—by both Dolores and the gallery. Some of those vases are museum pieces. And they're displayed so tastefully. Is that Dolores's influence, or . . . ?"

I shrugged. "I'm not sure. I've never seen the gallery without Dolores being nearby."

"I don't blame her for feeling concerned about the shop: it's incredible. And so is Dolores. She ought to be working in an old-fashioned cigar factory."

"You saw it, too!" I exclaimed in delight. "I think of her as Carmen."

We gazed out at the street while chuckling over our like imaginings. The sun was hot, and waves of heat could be seen rising from the bright sidewalk. People surged past like a river bouncing over rocks. Tourists were easy to identify, for they wore shorts and halters and seldom protected their heads with hats. The residents knew better; they understood the strength of the sun.

Valerie spoke suddenly. "I'd love to design some dresses for that woman—long, with straight lines and a plunging neckline. Maybe a touch of jade here and there. Costumes for a sorceress!" She laughed self-consciously. Yet I felt sure she was not aware of the appropriateness of her description. I had felt the evil in Dolores before—yet when I tried to get it into focus it seemed to fade, and she was just a good worker, my husband's trusted partner in a profitable business.

Valerie took a sip of coffee. "I should think your husband would want you to handle the gallery. You have an elegance that's missing in Dolores. Have you ever considered it?"

"Oh, of course. I love art, and I've always felt a need to be useful. I'm not really comfortable being the grande dame. When Lorenzo and I were first married I went there a lot. Then, one day when Dolores was out for a few moments, I made a big sale. I was so proud of myself!"

I laughed at the memory. "Lorenzo was furious! He was so angry I was really frightened. When he calmed down, he explained that it just was not acceptable for a nobleman to permit his wife to work. It shamed him in the eyes of his peers. He told me that in the past, even the nobleman himself was supposed to remain idle. Of course, when family fortunes began to shrink, that was changed. But wives are still supposed to carry on the tradition."

I raised my cup, deliberately extending my small finger in an affected gesture. "I'm supposed to be living proof that my husband is successful. Sometimes, I'll admit, it gets to be more than I can stand." I nodded in the direction of the gallery. "Especially when I see a woman like Dolores, doing all the things I'd like to be free to do. . . . "

Valerie looked concerned. "I suspect it's more than that, isn't it? Dolores doesn't look like the kind of person who wants to share authority."

"How right you are." I realized I had never spoken of my disappointment to anyone before. "So I've given up on the idea of helping Lorenzo in his business. Luckily, I do have another project that's just as interesting. Did I tell you I inherited Soledad from an aunt?"

"No. How exciting! Then it's your house, not Lorenzo's?"

"That's right. And I can feel the difference. Oh, I love Soledad. And I love the feeling that I can do whatever I want with it. So—" I smiled with delight. "—I'm decorating it over. The entire place! Not that it was poorly done to begin with—I never knew my Aunt Melina very well, but she had good taste. It's just that everything is a bit neglected. I'm having fun redoing the old pieces and putting them in top shape."

"That sounds marvelous. If you need any help I'll gladly give it. I've taken a few courses in decorating, you know." She paused, suddenly shy. "Of course, I don't want to push in where you want to be alone. . . . "

"Don't worry. You'll never be officious—like Dolores. You're much too nice." I rose, dropped some bills on the table and led the way back to the street.

Miguel was waiting at the door. I smiled when I saw him. He was obviously growing impatient.

When we were in the Mercedes again and on the road out of Palma, I leaned close to Valerie. I did not want Miguel to hear what I had to say. "We'll probably see Patrick, too, when we get there. I expect he'll stay with friends in Pollensa."

"Patrick? How wonderful!" She spoke in a normal tone, and I glanced up in alarm. Miguel had not moved, yet I was filled with concern. Had Miguel heard Valerie's exclamation? If he had, then Lorenzo would soon know that my brother had not stayed away. I felt as if a cloud had suddenly come over the sun. Lorenzo would be angry. And I had learned to fear his anger.

Chapter 7

Before my aunt died and left Soledad to me, I would never have considered it possible to fall so completely in love with a house. Maybe I had always remained detached from the places where I lived because my father moved around so much. Maybe I had learned to protect myself from a feeling of loss by avoiding any special affection for any one location. I know only that I grew up with a feeling of being at sea—with no home port toward which to set sail.

Soledad gave me that place to anchor. My aunt was a stranger to me. I had seen her once, during a short visit she made to France while my father was stationed near Paris. Her husband, a wealthy Greek ship-builder, had just died, and she seemed very alone. I was a child, and I had accepted her without question. When she returned to her home, she seemed to have recovered.

For a few years following her visit I received a gift from her each Christmas, but then they stopped coming and I forgot her completely. Until the day I was notified of my inheritance.

I was living at the time in a small apartment in Versailles, on the outskirts of Paris, where I had moved

to be close to Patrick after Alan's death. I still felt
depressed, and very much alone, in spite of Mimi
and my brother. The unexpected legacy sparked my
imagination. Imagine me, the grand lady in an estate
of my own! And in Majorca—land of sunshine and
adventure! I had never before set foot on any of the
Balearic Islands.

I departed as quickly as possible for Soledad. It had
been a cold, rainy day in Paris, but the sun was warm
and bright as I first set foot on the quiet, gently sloping
land that was my inheritance.

As I watched Valerie lean forward in excitement so
she would not miss any of the lovely countryside
through which we passed, I was reminded of that
day three years before. I had been eager, too. And
little Mimi had bounced on the seat beside me.

"How far is it?" Valerie glanced at me and then
returned immediately to studying the scenery.

"As far as we can go. Roughly seventy kilometers."
I followed her gaze. "It's too bad the almond trees
aren't in bloom. They're so exquisite."

"That's all right. Those endless fields of poppies
are magnificent! And isn't that lavender?" She pointed
toward a large square of purple blossoms.

"Yes, it is." I was pleased that she seemed to be
enjoying herself so much. "You're well acquainted
with flowers, aren't you? Did you study botany, too?"

"Yes, some. It helps me in my art to know what
flowers exist. I had to draw lots of them for credit in
the course." She nodded toward the long mountain
range that seemed to rise from the roadside and stretch
up into the sky. "Do we go up into the mountains?"

"No. Sorry. We'll stay close to the base, though.
Is geography another one of your favorites?"

"Oh, goodness, no. When you first spoke of Majorca, I thought it was a big, flat section of land near
southern Spain. I never expected mountains as beautiful as—" she paused while Miguel maneuvered us

past a minor accident "—as they are. It's really a surprise."

We entered and left a small village slumbering under the shade of a eucalyptus tree so large I feared it might break in two. A cluster of children paused in their play and waved as we passed. I caught sight of one name on a milestone: Santa Maria. A few moments later we were through Binisalem and Inca.

Miguel slowed down as we approached the fork. "Alcudia? Or Pollensa?"

I nodded toward the left. "Alcudia, please. We'll go through Puerto, and have a better view of the ocean." I turned to Valerie. "The Bay of Pollensa will be marvelous this time of day. It's like a sapphire when the sun begins to set."

Val pressed closer to the window. When the bay came into view she gasped with delight. It was, as always, a spectacular sight. The sharp peaks that surrounded it were a peculiar shade of gray, devoid of vegetation. In my imagination I pictured the moon like that.

Valerie could not look away from the sight. "I'm going to start painting . . . I have to. The colors here are absolutely unbelievable!"

I uttered a silent prayer of thanks. At least she had not said "painting, too"! Miguel might have noticed the inference and become convinced that Patrick was back. As it was, I could still hope that he hadn't noticed Val's earlier mention of Patrick's name, and that, though my brother was on the ferryboat with Valerie, he had managed to remain out of Miguel's sight.

We traveled along the harbor in silence, too wrapped up in the view to bother with conversation. There was little activity to distract us. The hotels along the waterfront were quiet and only a few yachts and fishing boats remained in the harbor.

As soon as we were through the village, we turned onto a dirt road that led up to a wide, flat plateau.

Vegetation hid our view of the surrounding country, and every so often we roused a bird from its nest in the brush. It flew upward, screaming raucously, startling me so that I jumped. It was as if we were suspended between earth and heaven. Civilization had been left behind.

"I'm beginning to understand why this place is called Soledad. . . . Solitude—a perfect name."

"It is pretty, isn't it? Now you can see why Lorenzo thought you'd be wise to bring your car. Whatever we want—even if it's just a simple purchase—we have to start by driving this road."

As I finished speaking, the house came into view. Miguel turned down the cedar-lined approach road and came to a halt in the courtyard formed by the three wings of the great mansion.

"Mommy! Mommy!" As we got out of the car, Mimi came racing across the lawn, her blond hair flying out behind her. She reached us at full tilt and leaped up into my waiting arms. For a time I devoted myself to receiving kisses of welcome, delighted to see my daughter again. When she grew calm, I put her down, facing Valerie. "Mimi, this is Valerie Roberts. You'd better call her Miss Roberts. She'll be your teacher."

Mimi turned suddenly shy. She curtsied and extended her hand. "Pleased to meet you. Miss Roberts."

Valerie took her hand. "Why not call me Valerie. I think Miss Roberts is a bit too formal."

Mimi considered her words and then smiled. "Take me to the beach?"

"Now?" Valerie looked at me, and I nodded. It would be a pleasant way for them to get acquainted. "All right!"

"Do you know how to swim? I have to use a life jacket because mommy thinks I'm too little."

"I think she's right. There'll be time enough for you

to go out on your own when you get older. Isn't the water rather treacherous? It looks deep."

"It isn't all over. There's a tiny beach, just big enough for us. I'll show you how to get there." Mimi took Valerie's hand and began to pull her toward the shore. "Do you know the breaststroke? I'd like to learn it."

I heard Valerie's clear laugh as she moved away. "Yes, Mimi, I know the breaststroke—and I'll teach it to you as soon as my cast is removed. I had lots of cousins who wouldn't let me play with them until I could keep up with them."

"Uncle Patrick started to teach . . . ." The rest of what Mimi had to say was lost. Valerie swiftly took the child's shoulder and guided her toward the beach. Already she had learned to conceal the mention of that one forbidden name. I glanced toward Miguel, but he showed no interest in our activities. He had removed Valerie's baggage and was preparing to take it up to her room.

As he headed for the steps, Eulalia, the cook, appeared. Behind her came Amparita and Incarnation, the two young girls who, according to the custom of the village, were spending a year working in the "big house," where they would learn to keep the floors clean and the beds made. By the next spring they would be married, and other girls would take their places. This was a sort of apprenticeship I had inherited with the estate. I saw no reason to alter the custom, for to me it seemed very charming.

"Will Señor Santos be along, too?" Eulalia's mind was already busy, planning the evening meal for her unexpected guests.

"No, Eulalia. Probably not until tomorrow. He's staying in town to make sure Miss Roberts's car is all right. Its brakes were fixed in Paris, before she came here."

"Thank you, *señora*." Eulalia disappeared into the darkness of the house. Amparita followed. But Incarnation stepped lightly to where I stood and leaned close.

"Señora Crystal, Dr. Reyes came by this morning. He said he expected you to arrive soon, so cook is all prepared. She just likes to make it look as if she's done everything on a moment's notice."

I grinned. The girls were obedient when Eulalia gave an order, but they still liked to show their independence. "Thank you, Incarnation. Did he have anything else to say?"

"Yes. He asked that you go to see him in Pollensa—when you arrived." She paused. "He said morning would be all right, if you got here too late."

"Thank you." I watched as the girl scurried after her friend. Then, almost guiltily, I glanced at Miguel. Had he heard Incarnation? He gave no sign. And he nodded a greeting to Incarnation as they passed. He would be putting the car away for the night and would probably spend much of his evening wiping it clean. I could tell he hated the dust on the unsurfaced road.

I headed slowly toward the house, grateful that the doctor had left the message that tomorrow would do as well as today. It was already growing dark and I was too tired to hike the three miles into town. I certainly didn't want to rouse Miguel's curiosity by taking my own car out instead of just asking him to drive me where I wanted to go.

Tomorrow would be best. Especially if Lorenzo did not arrive until well after noon.

Chapter 8

Lorenzo came early the following morning. Valerie was delighted to see her car running so smoothly, and she thanked him profusely. He accepted her thanks in silence and when she was finished strode quickly into the house. "I'll stay for lunch, then Miguel will drive me back to the city. Don't feel in any hurry to follow. I think it might be good for you to get a long rest here, in the house you love. Dr. Shabib said you were recovered, but I don't want to put you out of sorts again, just because we were eager for you to be fully over your trouble."

I did not argue, though I felt a disappointment at the thought that he would remain in Soledad until past noon. I had no doubt as to what Dr. Reyes had to tell me. Patrick would be staying with him, and he would want to arrange for us to meet. Of all the residents on the island, only Dr. Reyes showed sympathy with Patrick during his trouble. He was a friend worth having.

I could not deny that I was curious about my brother's return. Had Patrick discovered some way of proving his innocence? He had been unable to prove that he was not the culprit when an expensive art piece was stolen. Only Lorenzo's intervention kept him from going to prison. I had been told very little about the circumstances, and Patrick had been hurried away before we had time to talk. Now we could reach an understanding.

I spend most of the day arranging things in the house, checking what had been done during my absence and issuing orders for future work, while Valerie and Mimi roamed the estate. Val was hardly handicapped at all by the new, lighter cast; her energy easily matched the child's, and I was pleased to see how well they got along. I had been worried that Mimi might resent having additional supervision. She had spent too many years with the freedom to come and go as she wished.

The estate was mostly uncultivated, though at one time peasants had farmed the land. Now it was wild and totally untamed, in some ways reminding me of the open land near Old Saybrook, where I had spent so many happy summers. I could see that Valerie was delighted with everything she encountered.

I actually owned a small valley between two hills as well as the shoreline, most of which was quite rocky. At one point the land sloped down to a tiny beach—Mimi's favorite playground. The only part of the entire estate that was cultivated was the walled garden, and that was carefully tended, for it provided us with many of our fresh vegetables and fruits.

True to his original plan, Lorenzo left shortly after lunch with Miguel at the wheel of the Mercedes. I watched them depart with a feeling of relief. Since we didn't have a telephone there was no way of notifying Dr. Reyes that I would be late, and I worried that he might become upset at my delay.

Unfortunately, I dared not rouse the curiosity of the servants, for though they worked for me, I suspected that they felt a greater loyalty to Lorenzo. He was, after all, a "grand *señor*," one of their own. I was a foreigner. And I had been ill. The doctor had given his message to Incarnation, that was true. But I still did not trust her completely. I did not want to put her in a position of knowing secrets that might get her in trouble with Lorenzo—or with Eulalia.

So I waited through the day. As a special celebration of my return, I scheduled dinner early, so Mimi could eat with Valerie and me. She was delighted, and she chattered merrily the entire time, informing me of every path she and her new teacher had taken during their explorations.

Valerie seemed as excited as her charge. "Crystal, I'm impressed! Mimi took me up to the top of a hill and showed me the harbor. Are all three of those boats yours?"

"Mine—and Lorenzo's. They come in handy during the hot summer months, when I have company at Soledad. Much of the time I do my shopping by boat, in Puerto. It's just around the cape. Remember? We went through it on the way in."

Valerie nodded. "Miguel said something about Pollensa. Is it on the sea, too?"

"No, it's inland. If there's a storm at sea, or if Lorenzo is out in the cruiser, or if I just don't feel like sailing or taking the little Criscraft, I can take the car to Pollensa. We don't get many storms here, fortunately, but those we do get can be terrible. When Patrick did the shopping, before he left the island, he usually preferred to go inland. He . . . ." I paused. Amparita had arrived, carrying a special dessert.

Mimi bounced with delight. "Eulalia didn't tell me she was making my favorite cake. Oh, mommy, I'm so glad you're back!"

I couldn't help but smile. Everything seemed to please my effervescent daughter, and I was thrilled to be sharing her experiences once again. We ate the dessert in silence, relishing its sweetness. When Amparita returned with two cups of espresso, I nodded to Mimi. "Time for you to go to bed. Go along now. Simone will be waiting in your room."

"Please, mommy? Just a little bit longer?" She clutched at Valerie's hand, looking for support.

"No, darling. Valerie must be allowed some time to herself. You'll see her tomorrow." I folded my napkin. "Kiss me good-night."

She made no further attempt to extend her day, but kissed my cheek, and Valerie's, as well, then left for her room. I rose. "Valerie, if you're not too tired from hiking around with Mimi, I'd like to show you the remains of an Arabian palace that once stood on this property. There's not too much left, but you can see how big it was. At least three times the size of this place—and the gardens were magnificent. They even had a maze! Of course, it's all run-down now. But the mirror of the moon is still there."

"The mirror of the moon?"

"A pool designed to reflect the moon on certain dates important to the Islamic religion. Muslim architects were often poets, as well."

I could see that I had roused her interest. "It's not too late, is it?"

I shook my head. "Not at all. The sky stays light long after sunset. If we leave right away . . . ." I didn't have to continue. She was beside me, cane in hand, ready to depart.

As soon as we were out of sight of the house, I turned from the main path and followed a narrow trail that led through a hill of large boulders. We moved swiftly, for though the path was narrow it was not steep, and Valerie had little trouble keeping up. "Where is this place?" she asked as we reached the top of the first rise. "I thought it was near the kitchen garden."

"No, it isn't. I said that for the benefit of Amparita. She reports everything she hears to Eulalia. We're going up the hill and over to Pollensa." I paused as

I clambered over a large boulder. "Dr. Reyes, a good friend, sent a message for me. I think Patrick might be near, and I thought you might want to see him again."

She quickened her pace. It was quite clear that Patrick had interested her far more than she was willing to let on.

We reached a level plateau and at last arrived at the road. I turned onto it, confident that we were well out of sight of the house. Valerie moved up beside me so we could talk.

"There are actually two farms on my property," I began. "But they're both some distance from the house. One is on the other side of that hill over there. It's run by a family of native Majorcans who raise grapes, wheat and olives—mostly for sale in Pollensa. The other farm is nearby, in that hill above the town. It's abandoned, and almost in ruins."

"Are we going there now?"

"No. First we'll go to see Dr. Reyes, since he's expecting me. But I suspect that Patrick is hiding up at the old farm. He's always liked that place, and now . . . ." I did not bother to go on. The village was in sight, and I quickened my pace. If we had to go to the farm to meet Patrick, we would have to hurry. I didn't mind heading home in the dark, but I did want Valerie to see what a lovely place it was.

Dr. Reyes greeted me warmly. He had treated me when I had my breakdown—I remembered that now—and it had been on his recommendation that I was sent to the clinic in Paris. I embraced him fondly.

"Don't waste your time with an old man." He smiled warmly and kissed my cheek. "Not tonight, anyway. You'll have time for that another day. Now hurry up to the farm. Patrick is staying there for the time being."

I could not leave quite that abruptly. "Doña Catalina is well?" Doña Catalina, the doctor's sister, was also a good friend, and lately her health had been failing.

"Fine, just fine. Oh!" He saw Valerie in the dusk behind me. "You have a companion."

"Yes. Dr. Reyes, this is Valerie Roberts. She's an old friend—from my childhood—and she's come to tutor Mimi."

"Good. Well, run along." He reached out suddenly and took Valerie's hand in his, bringing it to his lips in an old-fashioned gallant salute. "Delighted to have met you *señorita*. Another time we must talk a bit."

"Thank you, yes." Valerie turned and followed me down the walk. "Have you known Dr. Reyes long?"

"Only since I came here. He used to be my aunt's doctor. When I moved here, he became mine—and Mimi's. Actually, he's the only real friend I've had on the island—except for Patrick, and now you."

She strode beside me up the road. "Please, I'm really confused. Why is Patrick hiding? I know you told me a little about it, but not all."

The light was fading, and I quickened my steps. I had a flashlight in my pocket, but I preferred not to use it until it was absolutely necessary. I began my story slowly.

"During the first year of my marriage to Lorenzo, Patrick spent only a few days with us because he didn't want to impose on Lorenzo's hospitality. He'd come down from Paris, where he was taking some special course in the use of acrylics, and visit us for a few days, and then he'd go back."

I paused for a moment. Somehow it was important that I keep things in proper order. "Anyway, I guess it was shortly after I tried to work in the store and got Lorenzo so angry. I was left alone a lot more than at the beginning—and I began to miss Patrick very much. Really miss him! So I invited him to stay at Soledad with me when he finished his class. There are lots of jobs available here for artists: painting portraits of visitors and tourists—things like that. I knew he would find work, especially in Pollensa. It's quite a tourist attraction.''

Valerie stopped briefly to rest her leg. "Did Mr. Santos approve?''

"Well, he didn't object. So after a while I thought Patrick might be able to work at the gallery. We both received a decent inheritance when father died, but Patrick spent most of his money on canvases and classes in special techniques.''

The climb was steeper, and I had to pause for breath. "I must admit, I was surprised when both Dolores and Lorenzo approved of the idea. Dolores arranged a studio for Patrick at the rear of the gallery.''

"How did Patrick and Dolores get along? She doesn't strike me as the type to like people around her who are independent, and he seemed to me to be—''

"The wrong kind of person—right? Well, surprisingly enough, they got along quite well, though he did complain at times of her moods. Still, she has a good head for business, and when she saw how good he was, she suggested that the gallery might offer restoration facilities.''

"Restore old paintings? Can Patrick do that? I know it takes special training.''

"Well, trust Patrick to have taken enough courses in the technique to be very good at it. I wasn't surprised; he's always been talented at repair work. He has the necessary patience. He can even duplicate a painting if he wants to—down to the last brush stroke.'' Realizing that I might be giving the wrong impression of my talented brother, I added, "Don't misunderstand me. He's a good painter on his own, too. His style is quite distinctive. When we get home I'll show you a portrait he did of Mimi.''

"So what happened? How could anything go wrong with such an arrangement?''

"I don't know exactly. Everything went so well, until . . . ."

The path took a turn ahead, and beyond we could see the dark outline of a farmhouse. There would be no time for me to finish the story, that I knew. So I made no further attempt. Instead, I caught Valerie's arm. "Please. Patrick is in there waiting for us. He'll tell you the rest. It sounds incredible, but I promise you what he says will be the truth. I believe him, even though there's no way he can prove it."

I released her arm and led the way to the door. The building was dark—and deathly quiet. But before I could knock, the door opened and Patrick stood before us. "Crystal! I hoped you'd get here soon. It's a little risky, my staying here, but I had to see you. And—" he turned to Valerie "—the lovely lady I met on the ferryboat." He bowed in mock gallantry. *"Bonsoir, mademoiselle."*

Val blushed and laughed, holding out her hand. "Hello, Patrick." She met his eyes squarely. "I should be angry with you; you didn't tell me the truth, you know. Pretending you didn't even know your own sister!"

He made a face. "So, sue me! And here I went to all this trouble to show you that there still are places on the island that are unchanged." He strode across the room and lighted an old lamp. "See? Authentic antique. And the cobwebs—guaranteed at least fifty years old. And the dust!" He burst into laughter, and we both joined in. "Come to think of it, I'm quite a rarity myself: a proven forger who's never been sent to prison!"

Valerie looked shocked, and Patrick turned to me. "You didn't tell her? Good Lord, she must think I'm insane!"

"I'm sorry, Pat, I didn't have time. But I started. I got as far as where you were doing restorations." I turned to Valerie. "We were really so happy about

it all. Everything seemed to be going so smoothly."
I faced Patrick. "I thought you'd like to tell the rest
yourself."

"Tell it? Yes, I can do that. But explain it? Never!
How can I when it makes no sense? It's driving me
mad. Crystal, I came back because I can't let it be. I
just can't. I did nothing wrong. . . ."

I glanced at Valerie. "Please, you'd better make
some sense. Valerie is getting very confused."

He turned to her then, and their eyes met. I knew
my brother well and never had I seen him so intense.
"Valerie, I'm sorry to drag you out of the house like
this, but I had to tell you what happened. I just couldn't
stand having you hear Lorenzo's side first." He paused
and scratched his head. "Sorry, I just don't know
how to begin." He sighed. "Well, here goes. . . . Last
September Señor Peraldez, a very wealthy man and
a regular customer at the gallery, moored at Palma
during a cruise of the Mediterranean. He's a beef
baron in Argentina, and supposedly a serious collector of art. He brought in a Picasso painting that had
been damaged to inquire about having it restored.
I'm not quite sure how it was stained. He said something about a storm that had torn the painting from
a wall and thrown it onto a table full of food and
drink."

He was speaking more smoothly, and I could tell
that Valerie was interested. He went on. "It really
was a mess. The frame was broken and the can-
vas was torn and soiled. It wasn't a pretty sight, especially when you consider how valuable it was."

"Crystal told me you were very good at restorations."

He shrugged. "It didn't help me much this time.
While I was working on the restoration, I got to like
the painting a lot. The colors were bold and the lines
so clean and well defined. So just for fun, and, I
suppose, because I rather relished the idea of having

a good copy of a work of art I honestly admired, I
made a copy. Then, because I was proud of my work,
I asked Dolores and Lorenzo to tell me, just from
looking at the two paintings, which was which."

He smiled. "It was really quite complimentary. They
both chose my copy. We made a great joke of it. I
remember Dolores said I had a promising career ahead
of me—as a forger!" He shook his head, as if unwilling
to believe what followed. "So after that I carefully
crated the original. Mind you, I made sure it *was* the
original. Then I put my copy in a closet, along with
some other paintings I had done through the summer." He paused. "Please don't think I only make
copies and repair other people's masterpieces. I wield
a smart brush myself."

"Yes, I know. Your sister told me." Valerie spoke
so quietly I hardly heard her.

"Well, later I want you to see for yourself." He was
clearly concerned that she think well of him. "Anyway, the next night Peraldez called to say he was
ready to sail. He asked me to bring the painting to
his yacht. I was pleased; I've never been in one of
those floating palaces, and I wanted to see what it
was like. So I took the crate and went to the harbor."

"What did you do between the time you showed
your copy to Lorenzo and Dolores," I interjected,
"and the time you delivered the painting? You have
to remember. I'm sure it's important. Did you leave
the crate in your studio?"

"Please, Crystal, you should remember that. I came
out here—to finish the portrait of Mimi. I stayed
overnight and returned to Palma late the next afternoon, just in time to get Peraldez's phone call."

"Go on," Valerie urged him to continue.

"Well, around ten o'clock that night I took the painting to Peraldez, as was arranged. I suggested that it
be uncrated immediately and hung, but Peraldez had
seen it at the shop and assured me he was very pleased

with it. He said he didn't want to run the risk of further damage should they encounter another storm on the way back to Argentina."

He was silent for a while. Then abruptly he started again. "The trouble is, he didn't sound convincing. Honestly! He said something about wanting to hang the painting in his ranch house, to show his friends that a rancher could also be an art lover. But it sounded phony! I was disappointed. I felt convinced that he only considered the painting important because of the investment. You know—a Picasso."

He stopped again, his brow furrowed, and for a time it looked as if he would not continue. At last Valerie spoke up. "What did his yacht look like? Was it as elaborate as you expected it to be?"

He seemed relieved at the change of subject. "Oh, it was really great—just like the pictures. Like a movie set, I guess. I kept expecting a star to come in, dripping wet from a swim in the bay." He smiled. "Thanks. I can go on now. You see, two days later, without any warning, Peraldez was back in Palma. He was furious! He had the Picasso with him and was waving it around like a madman. I was a thief, he shouted. I had given him a cheap copy!" His voice sounded hollow. "The terrible thing is, he was right: the painting he had *was* my copy."

"But you said you put it in your closet. How could it—"

"I don't know how. If only I did! And you should have seen Lorenzo's face— And Dolores's. It was terrible! I ran to my closet, but there wasn't any Picasso there. What I mean is, the original wasn't there, just the other paintings of mine. I didn't know what to do. I expected someone to call the police. And I couldn't understand how it had happened. . . ."

Neither Valerie nor I spoke. When Patrick continued, his voice was bitter. "Oh, Lorenzo was brilliant! He never even looked at me. He calmed Peraldez

down, offered him his choice of any two paintings
in the gallery. He even presented him with two Utrillos—at least as valuable as the Picasso, if not more
so. I could see his intention: he wanted to keep Peraldez quiet at all cost. His reputation as an art dealer
could be ruined by such an 'accident.' "

"Was it an accident, do you think? And if it was,
what happened to the other copy—the original?"

"Oh, I don't know! I honestly don't know. But there
I was, accused of being a thief, and Lorenzo was
preoccupied with saving the reputation of his gallery.
He didn't even consider the possibility that I was
innocent. I was furious. I demanded a police investigation."

Again he paused, and I could see he was reliving
the trauma of those days. "Lorenzo refused to call
the police. Refused! Peraldez had quieted down and
was really quite content with the Utrillos. I was right,
you see—he didn't value the Picasso except as an
investment. Lorenzo Santos had paid dearly to protect
the reputation of his gallery. He didn't care at all for
what had happened to my good name—or to my
integrity. Not an iota! He was cold as ice toward me
when Peraldez finally left, and informed me that if
I still had a shred of honor I would take my Picasso
and leave the island. As far as he was concerned, the
matter was closed. In fact, he informed me that he
considered me no longer welcome in his house—or
at Soledad."

Valerie seemed to share my brother's distress. She
asked gravely, "Patrick, was it your idea to make the
copy?"

"Certainly. Well, you see, I'd been doing it every
once in a while, when there was some painting one
of us particularly liked. I'd made a copy of a Van
Gogh for Dolores to hang in her home. I must confess
I was a bit surprised when she asked me to do it. She
generally didn't like anything that wasn't genuine.

But still, what I did looked authentic—if you didn't study it too closely."

"So that was when you left the island?"

"Yes. I left here about two months ago. But I couldn't stay away. I had to come back and find the original. I'm sure it would help me solve the puzzle." He shook his head. "I can still hear the accusations Peraldez shouted when he came back. He called me a lying thief. He said he could see what I had in mind; that I'd decided it would be easy to fool a rough ranchman from South America. No one would ever question the authenticity of the Picasso in the woods of Argentina. Then later, when things quieted down, I'd produce the original and sell it to some unscrupulous collector who would be careful not to ask how I got it. He even intimated that I might have made the switch on assignment from some rich man who had seen the painting on his yacht. He suggested that I might have been doing this for a living! That I had come to the island so I could take advantage of Lorenzo's gallery to make my exchanges!"

He turned toward me. "I never told you this before, Cris, but he even accused you of marrying Lorenzo just so I could get close to the gallery. Imagine!" He swung his fist in the air. "I felt like hitting him. But of course that would only have made things worse."

"If Peraldez wasn't a real art lover, and your copy was so much like the original, how did he ever find out?"

Patrick shrugged. "I don't know; just luck, I guess. I had put on a new frame, since the old one was ruined, and he . . . well, he evidently decided to look at the painting after all, just in case he didn't like the frame. And then he didn't. So he stopped at Barcelona and took it to another gallery there to have it reframed. While he was there he told his friend—the man who owned the gallery—about the accident, and how well the painting had been restored. He evidently was quite boastful. I guess his friend in Barcelona didn't have anyone who could do work like that.''

Valerie frowned. "I don't understand. How could changing the frame reveal that it wasn't a true Picasso? I thought it took some kind of spectrometer test.''

"Well, yes, that's what art museums use. But there's a very basic test that anyone can use. Haven't you heard of the old pin test?''

Valerie shook her head. "I'm afraid I don't know very much about such things. I've done a bit of oil painting myself, but I've never actually taken courses in art. Crystal tells me you've studied extensively. . . .''

His smile was fleeting. "Yes, but none of it will do me any good if I can't clear this matter up. I'll have to do just what Peraldez accused me of doing—because no honest dealer will touch me or my work.'' He inhaled slowly. "Anyway, the pin test. Of course, it's not the sort of test one goes about performing on valuable old masters, but it can provide some quick answers when the authenticity of an oil painting is clearly in doubt. What you do is stick a plain straight pin into the painting. If it stays there, upright, the paint is fresh; less than two years old, as a rule. If it falls out, the paint is old. Usually, the pin will take off a tiny flake of dry paint from the surface of the work. In the case of the Picasso, the test worked. The pin stuck firmly in the oil, proving the painting to be a copy. The original was done in 1950, long enough ago for the paint to be completely dry.''

"So Peraldez immediately—''

"No, not right away. He brought in a second expert, and that man confirmed that the painting was a copy. That was when Peraldez came back to Palma. I must confess I'd have done the same thing. However—'' he hit one fist against the palm of his other hand "—I just can't understand it! I can see Lorenzo's point of view: there didn't seem to be any other explanation than that I was to blame. Still, I think he might have had more faith in me."

"So what other explanations might exist?" Once more, I was trying to find a logical solution to the puzzle.

"Come on, Cris, let's not go through all that again. I'm sure neither Lorenzo nor Dolores is involved. I saw how they reacted when Peraldez came in the shop: they were shocked! Just as much as I was. No, I'm convinced someone made the exchange when Dolores was occupied with a customer. Maybe two people working together. But who? I'd do anything if I could figure it out . . . anything!"

I realized that Patrick was staring at Valerie with a sudden intentness. His voice was low—as if he was no longer aware of my presence. "Valerie? It matters to me. Do you believe me? You don't think I'm guilty, do you?"

She met his eyes without flinching. "No, I don't. I'm sure there's some explanation. And we'll find it. We have to!" She smiled, and his face lighted up in response. "You can still call in the police, you know."

He shook his head. The moment of intimacy was past. "No. They'd want to know why I left the island. They'd be sure I was guilty, that I'd stashed the painting somewhere in Paris, and . . . it just wouldn't work. Besides, I'd be getting Lorenzo in trouble, after all. It wouldn't be fair to Crystal. Lorenzo's already paid a high enough price for my silence." Again he shook his head. "No, I've got to solve this myself."

"I'll help—if I can." Valerie reached out and touched Patrick's arm.

He seemed not to notice. He was reliving those terrible days once more. "I tried to stay on and conduct a search on my own. I knew the minute I took the ferry to the mainland I'd be as much as admitting my guilt. But that made it very difficult for Lorenzo. He was sure I was guilty, and I can see why. He felt

I had tried to ruin him—and I'd almost succeeded. He never said another thing about it, and he never repeated his demand that I leave, but that only made things worse. I could see, though, that he was not treating Crystal the same as he used to. I suppose that was natural. Maybe he half believed that she had worked with me to take advantage of him."

I interrupted, "Please, Patrick! I could handle it; it wasn't that difficult. And I knew he would get over it in time. I think he has already. He was so wonderful when he took me home from the hos—" I stopped.

Patrick met my gaze, his expression serious and sympathetic. "I know you've had a rough time, Cris, and I'm glad you're so much better. Dr. Reyes kept me informed of your progress, but . . . dammit, I feel so responsible for this whole mess!"

I protested, "My . . . breakdown didn't have anything to do with that, I'm sure it didn't! It was just an . . . accident. A coincidence."

"Sure. Just a coincidence. No, sister of mine, I know you too well. You just worried yourself into the hospital. And you'd do that a second time if things got bad between you and Lorenzo again. I don't want to risk that. I'd sooner leave everything just as it is. . . ."

I couldn't answer. Was he right? Was the commotion over the Picasso the cause of my breakdown? Something in the back of my mind said yes. But I could see no connection. I had been upset, that I knew. But upset enough to temporarily lose my mind? It didn't seem to fit together. There were still too many parts of the puzzle missing.

I tried to force the memory back, but instead I found the old headache returning. I put my hands to my temples.

Immediately Patrick was beside me. "Poor Crystal! I've done it again. I wish I could make you happy, instead of adding to your troubles. What bothers me is that you never answered my letters while I was gone. Were you that sick?"

"Your letters? Patrick, I never got one letter from you, not one. Neither before I went to the hospital nor afterward!"

He frowned. "So Lorenzo kept them from you. . . . That wasn't necessary. How could he believe that I'd write anything that would disturb you? I love you, too. I'm your brother!"

"I know, Patrick. And I'm sorry. I'm sure Lorenzo was doing what he thought was best. He'll probably give them all to me as soon as he's sure I'm all well again."

"I never should have gone. You needed me, and all I thought of was myself. I should have stayed until I found the real thief. I'm convinced it had to be someone who was very familiar with the gallery. A regular customer, someone who knew about my copy. And the exchange had to have been made while I was at Soledad finishing Mimi's portrait." He began to pace about. "When I think of all the forged paintings hanging in museums all over the world . . . ! Some of them are not done half as well as mine was. You know, it might never have been discovered. If only I had put it in a frame exactly like the original one! It's all my fault, after all."

"Please, Patrick, I don't think you're to blame. You can't go on taking the responsibility now." Valerie's voice was sharp. "We have to think. It still could be Dolores."

"Oh, I suspected her, even though she did act shocked. But there's no reason for her to do a thing like that. She wouldn't risk the gallery and her glamorous job just for the profit she could make from the sale of one painting on the black market. I know she'd make a lot of money—but it wouldn't be worth it. She gets a large commission on every painting and art object she sells. She lives very well."

"Could she have done it to point suspicion at you? To get rid of you?"

"Oh, no. We got along fine. She really liked the painting I did for her—and she even had a few of my originals in her home. Besides, if she'd wanted me out of the shop, all she'd have had to do was tell Lorenzo. He'd have let me go. It's her decision that counts in the gallery."

"And Lorenzo?" Valerie glanced at me as she spoke.

"Come on, now! Not Lorenzo; he isn't a fool. His business could be totally ruined by all this. No reputable dealer would take such a risk. The shop makes a fortune; he doesn't have any need to deal in black-market art."

Valerie was quiet for a moment. "Miguel?"

"He isn't smart enough. Oh, he's a bull, all right. But it would take brains to carry off a switch like that—and he hasn't the capacity. No, it's someone else."

Valerie's eyes widened. "Patrick, what if . . . whoever it is . . . knows you're back. Isn't it possible that your life might be in danger?"

For a while Patrick stared back at her, and then he switched his gaze to me. An expression of shock was on his face. When he spoke, his voice was low. "Yours could be, too. Both of you! Did anyone see you come here?"

I shook my head. "No. I told the servants we were just going for a walk in the garden."

"Oh, Crystal, that was foolish. They can look out the window and see you aren't there. Try to remember: did you see anyone on the road?"

I shook my head. "No. And the only person we talked to was Dr. Reyes. Surely you don't suspect him?"

"No, of course not. Are you certain no one followed you?"

I looked at Valerie. We had been far too busy talking

to listen for footsteps behind us. "Patrick, I don't know. Besides, if someone were following us, he wouldn't stay on the road. He'd keep in the brush, out of sight."

He looked terribly worried. "So you don't know. It's possible that someone knows I'm here—and knows, too, that you've talked to me. I must know something—a clue to the real thief. It's there in my brain, but I can't seem to recognize it. If only I could. . . ." He paused. "Maybe you'd better get back. And take care. If you're being followed . . . ."

We slipped out quietly, waiting to open the door until Patrick had put out the lamp. The night seemed terribly dark—and dangerous.

We dared not speak as I led the way down the hill to the plateau and from there back to the road. Nor did I dare to take the narrow path back through the garden. Patrick had been right when he said the servants could see soon enough that I was not in the garden. There was no reason for us to continue the pretense.

I stopped abruptly. "What is it?" Valerie whispered next to me.

"I thought I heard something." I remained frozen in my steps. There was no sound behind us. Then, with a cry, a bird roused itself from sleep and soared up into the sky. I gasped. Had it been startled by some silent foot? Was our pursuer so close to us?

The blood was pounding in my ears, and I wanted to hurry. Yet if I began to run, wouldn't I be admitting that there really was someone behind us? And Valerie must certainly be worn-out by now from the unaccustomed use of her injured leg; she was already lagging behind. I caught her hand and clutched it tightly. Whatever happened, we would be together. Maybe we were safe as long as there were two of us.

We reached the house without further incident. The servants were all asleep—or at least they pretended to be. I walked with Valerie to her room and then crept silently into my own. I had reached one decision: neither Valerie nor I must go out alone—ever. But what danger stalked us, I didn't know. Who wanted to destroy Patrick—and me? And why?

My head was throbbing, and my fingers clutched the sheet tightly under my chin as I lay in the bed. I knew, suddenly, that I had to retain my sanity. I dared not fall again into the never-never land of a mental breakdown. I had to be aware—and strong— to face my enemy.

Chapter 9

I rose early the next morning. I had slept little, but I was not tired. My fear was too great. Was it only a fear of my unknown stalker . . . if there even was one? I did not think so. My fear stemmed from something deep inside me. Something I had buried when I had my breakdown. Something that was now ready to burst forth.

In spite of Valerie's presence in my home I felt alone once more—and very vulnerable. And I did not want my friend to be a witness to my remembering. If she was unaware of the terror that hung over me, maybe she would be safe. She and Patrick—and Mimi. They were all that mattered to me. Those three. I dared not include them in this moment of awakening.

There were other two people on the islands whom I trusted. One was Dr. Reyes; the other was his sister, Doña Catalina. She lived on Minorca, the second largest island in the archipelago, and quite different from the opulent Majorca. Lorenzo had gone there with me in the first month of our marriage, but he hadn't liked it at all, though its capital, Cuidadela, is only a three-hour boat ride from the Bay of Pollensa. He'd hated its flat, arid landscape and likened it to a poor relation.

I felt quite the opposite. I loved the peace that lay over the quiet city. I walked for hours past the arcades that lined the sidewalks, and gazed through the half-open doorways that opened onto shadowy gardens steeped in mystery and filled with fragrant flowers.

Most of all I loved Doña Catalina's ancient mansion. It was made of solid stone, yet it was far from cold and forbidding. The warmth of her personality pervaded the entire house. Her servants reflected her fondness for others, and the number of cats that came to the back door for breakfast every morning proved that it was all life she loved—that anything that approached her with trust received love and care from the depth of her great heart.

She would have made a wonderful mother. But she had never married, and now she was alone—and old. We took a liking to each other immediately, and by the end of my first visit she assured me that I must consider her home mine.

"Come anytime, and stay as long as you want. Having you near is like having a daughter—at last."

I relished the old woman's openness. Something about her took me back to my childhood when, no matter what happened, I knew I had a place of refuge.

It was to Doña Catalina that I went with my problem. I felt that Dr. Reyes was already too involved. If whoever was responsible for the theft of the Picasso learned that Patrick was back and staying in Pollensa, the doctor might also become an innocent target for evil. Doña Catalina was safer—away from Majorca, where the danger seemed to be centered.

She was sitting up in her great chair when I arrived. "Come in, little Crystal. I've missed you! My brother told me of your sickness. I'm so sorry. Are you better now?"

I took a stool at her feet. This was where I always

sat when we talked. "Doña Catalina, I . . . ." How could I start? "Yes, I'm a little better. But I have this feeling. Something made me have the breakdown. Whatever it was, I've forgotten it—I suppose because it hurt too much to think about it. But it's here—" I tapped my head "—inside me. And I feel as if it's about to come out."

She smiled with her warm, compassionate eyes. "So talk to me, my dear. I won't let it hurt you, no matter how bad it is."

I was silent for a moment, then gradually I found the words. "When I came to in the hospital, I didn't remember anything. And now—" It burst out, suddenly, like water breaking down the wall of a dam. "I was at Soledad, a few weeks after Patrick's terrible experience with the Picasso." I had spoken to Doña Catalina when I learned of Patrick's problem, and she had urged me to be patient. Now I was thankful that she knew the background of my trouble. "I was very upset, and Lorenzo seemed quite impatient with me. Around noon, he announced that he was going in to Palma. He had an important client he had to see. I wasn't to wait dinner for him, nor worry if he didn't return. He'd stay the night at the Casa Juarez, and come back to Soledad in the morning."

"Did he do that often?"

"Oh, yes. There wasn't anything unusual about it at all. And I didn't think about it again, after he left."

She waited in silence while I gathered my thoughts. I continued a bit more slowly. "Well, that afternoon, the youngest boy on the farm broke his leg. Dr. Reyes was visiting you for the day, and as you know, there just isn't anyone else in Pollensa who can set a bone. So I offered to take the child to Palma, to the hospital."

"Yes. I remember how upset Cristobal was that he wasn't there when he was needed. My brother is too conscientious."

Again I was silent for a time, struggling to put all

the memories in proper sequence. "I left orders for
Mimi to eat with the servants, and then I left for
Palma. The doctor there decided he wanted to keep
the boy overnight for observation, which was all right
with me. I ate at a nearby restaurant and headed for
the Casa Juarez. Then on the way I passed a movie
theater and decided on the spur of the moment to go
in and see the film. It must have been at least midnight
when I got out." I stopped for breath. "I knew Lorenzo wouldn't mind if I didn't arrive until late. He
was often impatient when I barged in on his confer-
ences."

"Had you called him to tell him you were in town?"

"Oh, no. I hadn't had any time for that. I was alone
with the boy. His parents had to stay behind and get
their day's work done. And I didn't see any need to
phone, anyway. I had an extra key in my purse, so
I knew I could get in, even if Lorenzo was still out
with his client."

I was amazed at how steadily the memories flowed
back. Why they rushed out now, I could not say. I
only knew that I recalled every detail of that night as
if it had all happened only a few days before.

"Well, I didn't even bother to ring the front door
bell, or to park my car in the courtyard. I drove directly
around the back and parked just off the street. I let
myself in quietly. If Lorenzo was asleep, I didn't want
to wake him. I'd already decided to sleep in my own
room, rather than disturb him."

Doña Catalina smiled in sympathy. "You didn't
think he might have a woman with him? Men have
appetites women do not always understand."

"Maybe I thought of that. I don't know. At any
rate, I sneaked in like a little mouse and prepared to
go to sleep. But—" I felt the excitement building "—before I had undressed, I heard something
that was very strange. I heard the sound of a guitar."

Doña Catalina was silent, and I continued slowly.

"It was coming from downstairs, and I was curious. I thought if Lorenzo was entertaining his client socially, it might be nice to join them. So I went down the stairs and stopped at the point where I could see into his little side room, the one he seems to like so much. Then I saw him. I didn't dare go any farther. Doña Catalina, it was Lorenzo! And he was playing the guitar!"

"Is that strange? Many Spanish men play the guitar. Some better than others, but they all seem to enjoy it."

"Yes, I know. But I'd never seen Lorenzo play it before. I didn't even know he knew how. And then I was afraid to move, afraid he'd see me. Because there *was* a woman with him. I could see her skirt and one of her high heels. She was sitting beside him."

I was reliving the evening as if it was just happening. Yet I knew, as well, how it would end. "At last I did bend over a bit and I saw her face. It was Dolores. . . ."

The old lady looked thoughtful. "I've wondered about those two. He seemed too close to her for their relationship to be quite normal." Then she leaned toward me, her eyes filled with sympathy. "But, my dear, surely you did not let that upset you? A woman who marries a Spaniard must learn to expect his little peccadilloes. It would be wrong to break up a marriage just because your husband was unfaithful. . . ."

Why did I feel depressed at her words? In the two and a half years since Lorenzo and I were married, I had grown away from him. Or was it that he had grown away from me? I wasn't sure. Nor was I sure if there had ever been a true intimacy between us. What I was certain of was that I no longer cared what he did—as long as he did not hurt Mimi, and as long as he treated me with courtesy when we were together. Even the temporary warmth of companion

ship that followed my release from the hospital had
not really improved our relationship.

"What did you do then?"

"I crept down a little farther. Doña Catalina, I had
to know! Was that wrong of me? I'm not sure. Anyway, what I saw next was a total surprise. Lorenzo
and Dolores were not alone. There were two others
with them: Miguel, and Señor Peraldez. They were
sitting in a circle, slouched on the couches. The coffee
table was covered with glasses and bottles of liquor.
Lorenzo was singing for them in a lovely, deep voice,
and accompanying himself on his guitar. He had never
sung for me!"

Doña Catalina chuckled. "Is that all that's bothering
you, my dear? That he was entertaining his friends?
Maybe he feels hesitant about singing to you because
he thinks you might make light of his talent." She
patted my hand reassuringly. "It must have been a
relief to see that he was not carrying on with that
Dolores woman."

"I suppose I did find it a relief. But I didn't feel
pleased for very long. Oh, Doña Catalina!" I remembered it all at last. Every word—every nuance of
expression. The familiarity between the four conspirators. Because that was what they were: conspirators! I remembered how subservient Miguel always
was when they were in the public. None of that was
evident as they sat together in that room. He was
Lorenzo's equal—and he knew it.

"When Lorenzo stopped singing and playing, Miguel began to speak." I continued swiftly, for I no
longer had to search my memory; it was all there.
"He jabbed his finger toward Lorenzo. 'Come now,
Cisco' " I mimicked the chauffeur's gruff tones.
" 'We're all partners, don't you forget it! Partners
from the beginning.' I could tell by the slur in his
voice that he was drunk."

Doña Catalina continued to watch me carefully.

"You still haven't come to the part that shocked you into the breakdown, have you?"

I met her eyes. "No. But how did you know? I wasn't sure myself until I began talking."

"I can tell." She patted my hand again. "You're trembling, my dear. And your voice is shaking. If it's too much for you, why don't you wait. You can tell me later."

I shook my head. I had to go on. I had to say it all, so I would not forget again. And I needed her beside me while I recalled the painful memories, so I would not again seek shelter within myself from what I feared.

"I realized, suddenly, that Peraldez was the man who had been so angry at Patrick. He was the one whose Picasso had been stolen. It didn't seem right that he should be part of this confidential circle. Not right at all! I found out just how wrong it was when Dolores began to speak. 'Cisco, we've wasted enough time. I don't get the thrill out of drinking that you and Miguel do. I don't think Peraldez does, either. But you must admit I've been patient. Why you didn't just get rid of her at the first opportunity, I'll never know.' "

"Get rid of her? Did she mean you?"

"Yes, I think she did. I know she did. She turned toward the wall where my portrait hangs and made a gesture like a Gypsy giving a curse. Peraldez laughed and patted her shoulder. 'Take it easy, Dolores. You can't deny she's a striking woman. Let Cisco enjoy her for a little time before . . . .' He made a gesture with his hand across his neck. I was too startled to move. They were planning to kill me! The only thing that bothered them was that Lorenzo had not already taken care of it for them. . . ."

I waited until I was once more in control of my emotions. "Lorenzo tried to placate her. He poured her another drink, and he sat down beside her and put his arm around her shoulder. He told her that she ought to understand how important it was that he marry me. She just snorted, 'It was necessary then! But you've got what you need—what we all need. She isn't important anymore. She's in the way!' "

I could still feel the horror that had crept over me at that moment. "Honestly, Doña Catalina, I couldn't have moved right then if I'd heard them coming up the steps. Luckily, they didn't seem at all interested in moving. Dolores was so excited she was almost screaming. She said something about 'taking care of it herself, if Lorenzo didn't get moving.' She was tired of waiting. Tired of being a clerk in a stupid gallery. Tired of kowtowing to me whenever I dropped in. I'd never realized how much she hated me!

"I tried to creep up the steps, but I didn't dare to move. And then Lorenzo had had enough of her complaining. He stood up and faced her. I could see his face, and it was red with anger. 'Shut up, you little fool!' He screamed it. 'You've had too much to drink. You aren't thinking straight. So help me, if you don't take care, I'll forget—'

"Miguel interrupted him. He stepped between the two of them and pushed Dolores back onto the couch. Peraldez took Lorenzo's arm and led him back to his chair. Miguel shouted her down, because she wasn't ready to be quiet. He yelled something about her not making trouble for Cisco. He took her arm and sat beside her. He stroked her back and even kissed her cheek. I couldn't hear everything he said, but it was something about her being far prettier than I. He said she ought to know Lorenzo really loved her. She shouldn't allow herself to be jealous of a skinny snip like 'that blond female.' That's what he called me! And Lorenzo didn't turn a hair."

Doña Catalina was listening quietly. When I paused, she sat still, unwilling, I think, to disrupt my recollections. At last I continued. "Then Lorenzo took up his guitar again; I saw Peraldez give it to him. This time the others all joined in the singing—even Dolores. They sang some strange folk song I'd never heard before. I suppose it came from their home province in Spain.''

"Did you go back up to your room then?''

"Yes, after a while I regained my strength. I crept up to my little room and slipped back out of the house. I didn't dare to stay there. I was so very frightened. All I could think of was that Lorenzo wanted to kill me. That Dolores and Miguel and that man, Peraldez, were all in on the plot. I guess I must have wandered the streets, trying to sort things out, and apparently a policeman found me on a park bench the next day. I don't really remember anything much of what happened; it's all a haze to me still. I just know that I came to a month later in the hospital in Paris.''

Doña Catalina leaned forward and pulled me up into her arms. I crept close to her, like a hurt child wanting to be loved back to health. And I stayed close to her until at last my strength seemed to return.

The old lady sensed my recovery. "You're better now? Good! See, it didn't break you, after all. And now you know what you have to watch out for. Has there been any attempt on your life since you returned?''

"I don't . . . . No! But . . . .'' I paused, a new thought pushing my fear aside. "Oh, Doña Catalina, Patrick is back! I forgot one thing that one of them said—I don't remember which one. Something about 'now that that prying brother of hers is out of the way—' and then I didn't hear the rest. Patrick was framed, I'm sure of it! Why else would Peraldez have been there that night? He's one of them. Whatever it is they're up to, he's part of it all.''

Doña Catalina rose from her chair. "I wish I could offer a solution to your problem. But maybe you brought one with you. My brother tells me you've found a tutor for Mimi.''

"Oh, yes, Valerie Roberts. She's wonderful—good with Mimi, and a real companion for me. Patrick seems to like her, too."

"Well, you say you've had no attack on your life since your return. Maybe she has something to do with it. Maybe no one will touch you as long as she's around. At least for a while." She frowned. "I suppose you can't call the police?"

"What would I tell them? That I was afraid my husband was trying to kill me? He hasn't done anything to harm me—not yet, anyway. And if he wanted to, he could have me sent away again—this time to a full-fledged mental institution. No, I can't call the police." I brightened. "But maybe you're right about Valerie. We'll stick close together for a while. And I'll tell Patrick what I heard. Maybe it will help him solve the case. Now I'm sure Peraldez and Dolores knew all along that the Picasso had been switched. They must have done it themselves! Lorenzo, too; he was in on it. Because he wanted Patrick out of the way. But why?"

Doña Catalina pulled the cord that called for her maid. "Time for tea, my dear—and time to rest awhile. You've remembered enough for the time being. Don't push your mind too hard. Remember what the doctor said about taking it easy."

I did as she suggested. For the remainder of the visit I discussed unimportant things, like a new recipe for bread that she had promised to give Eulalia, and how well Mimi was doing in her studies.

On the way back I mulled over my new discoveries. I was no longer the half-aware creature I had been when I left the clinic. My memory was returning—and with it the terrors from which my mind had retreated. Maybe Lorenzo and Dolores—and the others—wanted me dead because of something I knew. Had I remembered it yet? Or were there even more frightening memories still hidden in my mind?

If there were . . . would I be able to pretend that I still recalled nothing? Would I make a slip in front of Lorenzo, Dolores or Miguel that would let them know I remembered? That I knew something they feared? And when I did, would they wait to kill me?

I searched the landing carefully before stepping on the shore. The return of my memory was a welcome event, but it marked a loss of innocence that meant my life would never again be the same.

Chapter 10

I opened my eyes slowly and stared around the room. The bright sunlight flooded every corner, as if defying any evil to escape its penetrating rays. I tenuously explored my inner being. I had lived with fear so long. Would it continue now until I ended my life in desperation? Or would my own husband beat me to it?

The fright was gone. Surprised, I searched again. No terror lay hiding to consume me. I was overcome with panic. Had I lost my senses again? Was I back in the clinic already?

I rose and stepped to the window. No, I was at home. The familiar garden of Soledad sparkled in the morning sunlight. I could hear Mimi and Valerie laughing together as they played at a game Valerie had designed to facilitate the learning of a foreign language.

Suddenly I needed some reassurance. That terrible story I had recalled so clearly when I visited Doña Catalina—had it been a fantasy? Had none of it really happened? And now that I had faced my nightmare, was I free to recognize it as nothing more than a bad dream?

I dressed quickly, humming a song from my childhood as I ran a brush through my hair and caught it in place with a barrette. Then I was down the stairs and out in the garden. "Valerie! Mimi! Where are you?"

Valerie called, and I ran to greet them. Mimi's face was flushed with excitement. "We've been playing a fun game, mommy! Listen, I can talk Italian!" She proceeded to name the flowers around her in a smooth, lilting voice. Then she described her actions in Italian, as well.

"That's very good. Valerie, you're a wonder—you've got her loving her lessons."

"She's a very bright child. She ought to enjoy learning." Valerie rested a hand on Mimi's shoulder. "Isn't it time for your morning rest? We're going to have a busy afternoon."

Mimi nodded, still smiling. "Yes, Valerie! Can mommy come with us?"

"If she wants to. Hurry along, now."

Mimi departed without any argument. I watched her run up the steps to where her nurse waited. "She's actually going to take a nap without a quarrel? Now I know you're good for us both! She's never been so docile with me."

Valerie smiled. "Thank you. This place—and you—are good for me, too." She began to walk toward the gate. "I think I saw Patrick signal from the top of the hill. Want to come with me and see?"

The fear returned for one moment. Was it really Patrick Valerie had seen? Or was this a trick to get me—to get us both—away from the safety of the house?

I had no time to voice my apprehensions. Valerie was already through the gate. I ran after her up the narrow path and over the hill. A small clump of trees nestled in a shallow ravine. As we approached, Patrick stepped out. "Val! Crystal! I hoped you'd seen me!"

Valerie ran lightly toward him, unmindful of her cast, stopping at last in his arms. It seemed natural for these two to be so comfortable together. Then I remembered that Patrick still did not know something very special about his new friend.

I feigned a frown as I reached them. "Patrick, you seem very familiar with a girl you hardly know!" But my act of annoyance didn't work. I burst into a grin as I finished.

Patrick was puzzled. "What do you mean, I hardly know her? What is there I've missed?"

"Just who she is!" I was laughing in anticipation of his surprise. "Ask her where she grew up."

He turned a questioning look at Valerie. She smiled. "I was born—and grew up—in Connecticut."

He looked at her intently. "Really? Not near Old Saybrook?" He continued to study her. "Valerie Roberts! Of course! I should have remembered—you're Mark Lefevre's cousin, aren't you?" She nodded. "I can't believe it! I used to tease you when you came across the river to play."

They laughed together. "I thought you were terrible!" Valerie told him gaily. "I remember you used to tease Mary, too. She told me once that you pulled her braids in school, when the teacher wasn't looking."

"Mary. Yes, that's right. She's Mark's sister, isn't she? And they had a big black dog! Where is she now . . . do you know?"

"In Canada. Married. Has two children of her own."

"And Mark? I remember Crystal had quite a crush on him. He rather scared me. He always acted so assured; seemed to know just what he wanted. Wasn't he studying to be a doctor?"

"Yes, and he is one. He's working in a clinic in Mexico."

"Well, what do you know! Strange, isn't it? No

wonder I liked you the first time we met. . . ." His
voice grew serious. "No wonder I love you now."

For one moment I was an outsider. Their eyes met,
and they kissed. Then he pulled her toward a fallen
tree and beckoned me to join them. "I had to see you
both—to tell you I'm leaving again. I have to go back."
He turned toward me. "I'm not running away again.
Honestly! It's just that I took a job in London after
I left here, assisting in the restoration of a wall painting. I had this week off because the man who's di-
recting the work was ill, and he wanted to be in on
everything that was done. But I have to go back now.
You understand, Crystal. And I'm glad I found out
why you didn't answer my letters. It still gets me
furious when I think that Lorenzo kept them from
you."

"Don't worry about it, Patrick. I'll find out about
them later. Will you be coming back?"

"As soon as the job is finished. Even if you and Val
weren't here, I'd have to return—to prove my innocence! I was lucky to get the work I did get; I'm sure
if Mr. Gadsworthy had known about this thing with
the Picasso, he wouldn't have hired me. I expect to
be back in a month or so."

He turned then to Valerie. "I'll write all my letters
to you, so Lorenzo won't realize they're from me. I'll
use the stationery with the museum's return address.
I suspect he might watch your mail, too, if he finds
out that we all practically grew up together."

Valerie nodded solemnly. "I'll write, too, Patrick.
Be careful. Take care of yourself." She touched his
cheek with her fingertips. "I'll miss you."

He embraced her again. "I'll miss you, too. And
I'm afraid you and Crystal are the two who will have
to take care. Something's wrong here, and I don't
know what it is. Who knows whether you're even
safe at Soledad. . . ."

Patrick rose abruptly and drew Valerie to her feet.

"I must go! The ferry leaves in an hour, and Dr. Reyes has agreed to drive me. He's picking me up just over the hill." He held her close for a moment. "Write to me often, please." He turned to me. "You, too, Cris. I'll be thinking of you."

Our farewells were short. He ran swiftly over the hill, as we watched. Then we turned and, hand in hand, descended to the garden gate. Neither one of us felt like talking. I could tell that Val was worried about Patrick. And I decided then that I would not add to her concern. I would try to stay near her, for my own sake and for hers, but I would not tell her of the conversation I had had with Doña Catalina. Between her work with Mimi and her anxiety over Patrick, she already had enough on her mind.

Later, when she had resumed her work with Mimi, I sat for a while in the garden, watching them together. In my mind was the memory of Patrick as he took Valerie in his arms. They already loved each other. And somehow I knew that they belonged together. I had felt like that with Alan—but we had so little time together. Would our love have been the kind that lasted? I would never know.

I had thought I shared that sort of affection with Lorenzo. Those initial weeks of our courtship were packed with excitement. After the terrible blow of Alan's death I was grateful, flattered, even thrilled to be once more the object of a man's attentions—especially a man like Lorenzo. But that romance had not endured. Lorenzo was a businessman, and it soon became apparent that I was no more than a wife of convenience. We shared nothing, meant nothing to each other.

Yet still I admired my husband. In fact, I was somewhat in awe of him. Although he chose not to share with me his innermost feelings, I saw he was a driven man and I respected his strength, which could amount to ruthlesness. To the degree that he saw fit he fulfilled his role as husband to me and father to Mimi, and it had not occurred to me to try to change him.

Even now, with the realization that I was an impediment to Lorenzo's mysterious plans—the possible victim of some evil scenario—my feelings about him were mixed. After all, what did I really know of his intentions? I had just recovered from a breakdown; perhaps my mind was distorting the images that haunted me, finding sinister patterns in meaningless, unrelated events. I was not yet ready to disrupt my life and Mimi's. My child was happy and secure at Soledad, the home I had never known. Most important, if I left Soledad, where would I go?

For the moment I was prepared to live with the danger. Valerie was with me, and Patrick would soon be back. . . .

As I reflected on my situation, I realized with a pang that I envied Val and Patrick. I regretted that I might die without ever fully knowing the kind of love they shared.

IN THE DAYS THAT FOLLOWED I found it easy to remain close to Mimi and Valerie. Dr. Reyes had removed Val's cast, so she was now able to enjoy increased activity with my ever rambunctious daughter. Her informal way of teaching was as interesting to me as to Mimi. We all learned together. We played together. And while we were together, I felt safe.

So safe, in fact, that I forgot to be careful. It happened on a bright Wednesday afternoon. Mimi was napping, and Valerie had set herself the task of writing to Patrick. I felt restless and so I slipped through the garden gate and headed for the road.

Most natives used the road when they walked, for there were few cars and everyone drove carefully. I trudged up the middle of the narrow gravel roadway, gazing idly at the bright blue of the bay with its changing shades and ever-moving patterns of light and dark.

It was as I was wending my way slowly back to the house that a noise behind me suddenly called me to an awareness of my vulnerable position. A car was coming. Still, I did not think of danger. I moved to one side of the road and continued with my dreamy viewing of the bay. By the time I realized the car was speeding, it was almost too late. I threw myself to one side just as the vehicle came upon me, and only because of this swift action did I avoid being hit. The car did not slow down, nor did the driver look back. When it was out of sight, I rose, dusted myself off and hurried home.

Had it been an accident? I had tried to see the car as it disappeared, but the dust had been too thick for me to recognize it. I had the feeling that it was white, and that frightened me. There was only one white car that I know of in the area—Lorenzo's Mercedes. But Lorenzo was in Palma!

When I reached the house, I felt my heart sink. The Mercedes was in the driveway, and Miguel was hurrying across the courtyard. Mimi had evidently awakened at the sound of the wheels on the gravel, for she was running down the steps to greet him.

I had never been able to understand the friendship that existed between Miguel and my daughter. With me he was very polite, but always reserved. He tolerated me because of Lorenzo. But he seemed to sincerely love little Mimi. Their relationship had been a good one from the first, when she was only three and a half and Lorenzo and I were still on good terms. Mimi had become tired as we walked along the shore, and had ordered Miguel to carry her. I had expected him to refuse, but instead he bent down and lifted her onto his shoulders. "You're a picador! Let's get the bull!"

Mimi had laughed with delight, grabbing onto

Miguel's hair as if it were reins and waving one arm as if she held a lance in her hand. "Olé!" Miguel shouted playfully, and dodged to one side. "Olé!" Mimi echoed, squealing with glee.

I watched Miguel lift Mimi into his arms. Had he tried to run me down? Could he have attempted to murder the mother of a child he obviously loved? What sort of man was Miguel? For that matter, what kind of man was Lorenzo?

As I asked myself this question, Lorenzo stepped from the car, a look of faint annoyance on his face. I stopped, afraid, suddenly, to greet him. If he had been the one trying to run me down, would he be able to face me?

He saw me and called my name. "Crystal! Where have you been? I came out to see how you are doing. Are Mimi's lessons going well?"

I did not reply. Never before had Lorenzo shown any interest in Mimi's studies. Valerie, who had followed Mimi from the house, answered, "She is doing very well, Señor Santos, thank you."

There was a moment of awkward silence. Mimi spoke at last. "We won't be able to go to Minorca now, will we?"

I shook my head. "I suppose not. But we'll go another day, don't you worry."

Lorenzo seemed to brighten. "You were planning to visit Doña Catalina?"

"Yes." I tried not to show my disappointment. "But we can do it another day. Mimi won't mind. There are many interesting things we can do right around here."

"Oh, but you mustn't disappoint the child. And Valerie. She hasn't met the lady yet, has she?" He saw me shake my head. "Well, then, is Doña Catalina expecting you?"

I hesitated. "Yes, she is. We made arrangements

for the visit by mail, a few days ago. She might worry if we don't arrive as we said we would."

"Well, then, you must go ahead. Don't worry about us. We can entertain ourselves." Lorenzo paused. "Actually, I just came out for a day's relaxation. I've been terribly busy lately, as you well know, and I'm beginning to feel the strain. I won't miss you. In fact, I'll rest better if I'm not disturbed."

I was aware of ambivalent feelings toward my husband. I could not help but resent the way he dismissed my company so casually. Yet at the same time I felt relieved that I could get away after all, for the near-disastrous incident on the road had shaken me badly.

Mimi was jumping up and down. "Oh, good! We can go! Come on, mommy, Valerie—let's hurry!"

I did not turn. "Lorenzo, I thought we'd take the Criscraft, if it's all right with you."

He shrugged. "Whatever you wish. I don't expect to go sailing."

"Fine, then." I felt desolate, gripped by confusion. Lorenzo seemed so distant—frighteningly so. Maybe he hoped the boat would capsize and we'd all three be lost at sea. He had not even noticed I was upset. Was that because he was the cause of my pallor?

"Lorenzo." I watched his expression closely. "I was almost run down on the road a few moments ago. Did a car race by you on the way? If I knew who it was . . . ."

He shook his head. "Miguel? Did you hear what Mrs. Santos said? Did we see a car pass us on the road? She says it was going fast."

Miguel shook his head. "No, Señor Santos." His face was expressionless. I turned back to look at Lorenzo. He, too, seemed unperturbed by my questions. But when he felt my eyes upon him, he became suddenly solicitous. "Are you sure you're all right now? You know, my dear, you might have imagined it. Most people don't drive fast on these roads."

I turned away. I would learn nothing further. If Lorenzo and Miguel had been my assailants, they were not going to let me know. They were too good at pretending innocence. "Maybe you're right." I tried to act convinced. "I guess I have been nervous lately." I turned to Mimi. "Are you ready to go?"

"We're going! We're going!" Mimi was dancing with delight. I took her hand and headed for the dock.

Lorenzo called out, "Will you be home tonight?"

"No, I don't think so. I'm sorry, if you had other plans for us. But Dr. Reyes told me Doña Catalina hasn't been well lately. I thought we'd stay the night there."

"That's fine." He seemed almost eager for us to depart. And pleased that we would not be back immediately. . . .

I felt a momentary uneasiness. But it vanished when Mimi tugged at my arm. "Please, mommy! Do we have to wait?"

"No." I continued down the path. "Lorenzo?" I glanced back. "Will you be here when we return?"

"I don't think so, Crystal. But don't worry. You're doing the right thing. Doña Catalina isn't getting any younger." He paused and then continued, "Be sure to give her my greetings."

"Yes." I forced my voice to sound cheerful. "Goodbye, then." He did not wait for us to reach the cove. When I looked back before descending the steps, he was nowhere in sight.

The small motorboat had been my favorite from the first time I used it, for I could handle the controls myself, and I found its power ample but not overwhelming. The cruiser was Lorenzo's choice whenever we went out together—or even when he went out on some errand associated with his business. I knew he liked the importance so large a craft afforded him; it impressed his customers. It had more speed, too, than the smaller craft, and both Lorenzo and

Miguel seemed to relish racing—even when there were no competitors to challenge.

Mimi searched the sea as we pulled away from shore. I had told her that we might see flying fish, and she was eager to show them to Valerie. But the surface water was not warm enough, so at last she settled back to watch the passing display of ships.

There were several in view. A large fishing ship was heading in from sea. Once I had taken Mimi down to watch the sailors depart, long before sunrise, and had pointed out that they returned to shore shortly after noon. She was delighted to see that I had spoken the truth. A small sailboat moved gracefully by, its sails billowing in the breeze. And then, from some distance away, the coast-guard cutter moved toward us.

I watched it for a time before I realized it was trying to overtake us. As soon as I understood, I slowed down and waited for it to draw alongside. A familiar voice called a greeting. "Ahoy, Señora Santos! It's Felipe!"

I introduced him to Valerie. Mimi greeted him like an old friend. She had seen him many times when he visited our kitchen.

"Is all well aboard?"

"Yes, thank you." I knew what he wanted to hear. "All's well at Soledad, too. Incarnation asked me to say hello if I saw you.

"*Muchas gracias, señora.*" He was pleased, as I knew he would be. "*Adios*, then." He waved. "Pleasant journey."

"*Adios*, Felipe. Thank you."

The coast-guard boat took off, slowly at first so as not to upset us. Then it increased its speed, and a white wake appeared behind it. Valerie followed its departure with her eyes. "What are they looking for when they sail around? Gold smugglers? Gunrun ners? Dope traffickers? Or do they just have to stay visible to show that they're working?"

"I don't think they're just going through formalities. They seem to be looking out for anything illegal. But Felipe was only interested in news of Incarnation. He wants to marry her, and her parents won't permit it because she's so young. He thinks of every excuse he can to come to Soledad on his days off, just so he can see her."

Valerie seemed to remember something. She pulled a letter from her pocket. "Oh, speaking of wanting to see someone . . . I got this note from Mark."

"Mark? How does he know you're here?"

"He doesn't. I left a forwarding address when I left Paris. Miguel brought my mail from Pollensa. I haven't even opened it yet."

I felt an inner excitement. Mark Lefevre! I hadn't realized he and Valerie corresponded.

Valerie tore the envelope open. She read in silence, smiling as she did so. Then she looked up. "How nice. He's taking a vacation—well, kind of a vacation—with a friend of his, and guess what! They've decided to tour the Mediterranean. Wouldn't it be a surprise if they came here?"

I felt lighthearted—filled with anticipation. "If they don't I'd be surprised! Everyone who comes to the Mediterranean visits Majorca. Is he just out for fun, or . . . ?"

"His friend is some sort of a marine biologist, so they'll be spending a lot of time searching the tidewaters."

I smiled with delight. "Then I know they'll be here—and maybe at Minorca, too. Some of the best tidewaters in the Mediterranean are around these islands."

"I wish I'd been able to contact them before they left Mexico." Valerie looked upset. "I did write Mark after you and I met in the clinic, but he doesn't mention my letter, so he must have left before it was delivered. What if we don't get to see him at all?"

I shared her apprehension. Yet I knew there were things I could do. "I'll drive into Palma when we get back to Majorca, and tell the harbor master to be on the lookout for his boat. Does he say what kind of vessel they're using?"

"What else? A sailboat—named *Cris*. He's never used any real name on any of his boats—don't you remember?"

I smiled to myself. So he still named his boats after me!

As we approached the private dock near Doña Catalina's estate, I was aware that Mimi was growing restless. I guided the boat into the slip and turned to Valerie. "How do you feel about taking Mimi into town for a while? We're still pretty early, and I'm afraid having an active child around for a long time might tire Doña Catalina. You can take the boat and come back closer to dinner. Is that okay with you?"

Valerie seemed pleased with my suggestion, and Mimi was delighted. I tossed a rope over the post and pulled the boat against the pier. Valerie slid into the driver's seat as I climbed ashore. "Mimi—" I tried to sound as serious as possible "—be good, now. Do what Valerie tells you."

"Yes, mommy. Can we buy a present for Doña Catalina?"

"That's a good idea." I pulled out some money and handed it to Valerie. "She loves teacups—fancy ones. Okay?"

"I'll do my best. What time shall we be back? Six?"

"I think that's about right. Have fun."

I waited until the small craft was out of sight. I could see that I was right to trust Valerie with the boat. I had assumed that anyone raised on the coast of Connecticut would know how to handle small boats, so I did not feel I was gambling too much. I knew **as** I watched that she was a skilled sailor.

I turned and walked up the path to the house. I had a personal reason for wanting to be alone right now. As always, I was eager to talk to Doña Catalina; she could help me recover my perspective as no one else could. But there was another reason, too—one I was not quite so ready to acknowledge. Mark Lefevre. The news in Mark's letter to Val had disturbed me, for I was not sure I was ready to see him after so long a time. Memories—sweet, confusing memories—of our relationship haunted me yet. And the knowledge that Mark still named his boats *Cris* told me that he remembered, too.

Chapter 11

Doña Catalina was lying on a settee in her room, and she did not rise to greet me. I hurried toward her. "Doña Catalina, are you ill? You look so pale."

"Nothing at all, my dear." Her voice was quavery; she seemed to struggle to frame her words. "It's just my angina acting up. Not important at all. I've had so many attacks lately—" her voice was steadier now, and she smiled "—the doctor doesn't even get excited by them anymore. But they're all very minor—not much we can do about it. I'm an old woman, after all."

I must have shown my worry, for she continued in a reassuring tone, "Just to show you how unimportant it is, my doctor left for the mainland this morning—for a few days. See? No reason for worry at all."

I studied her face. It appeared drawn, and her normally penetrating eyes seemed clouded with pain.

"Please, Crystal, wipe that expression off your face. Believe me, I'm fine. And for goodness' sake don't get all upset like Conchita, here. She practically passes out if I so much as complain of a pain. The doctor has given me some tablets for the pain—if it returns.

They help me to feel better almost instantly. I must say, I'm glad you're here. I'm not sure Conchita would be of much help if I did have any problems; she panics so easily." She smiled. "But I'm sure nothing will happen. Now—" she dismissed her troubles "—how are things at Soledad? Did you bring Mimi with you? And her new tutor?"

I explained that they were at Cuidadela and would arrive later.

"Cristobal, dear boy, seems quite taken by her. My brother always had an eye for a beautiful woman. He wrote me that all of you are in good health."

"Yes, fortunately."

"And are you happy? What we talked about the last time you were here—has it been settled?"

I wasn't sure what she meant, since I had left her with the reassurance that I would try to understand the meaning of my experience. Did she think I had talked to Lorenzo about what I had overheard?

She saw my confusion. "It was a nightmare, wasn't it? Just a bad dream?"

I understood. "Yes, that's all it was. I'm glad I got it off my chest. I feel better now." I pushed back a feeling of disappointment. I could not ask Doña Catalina for support. Not now. She was not strong enough to give help to anyone else.

"And Patrick? Is his problem settled, too?"

I could not lie about that. "I'm afraid not. He's gone away now for a while, but he'll be back in Majorca soon, and I'm afraid the trouble might start again."

"He'll solve the puzzle of the missing Picasso, I'm sure of it." She seemed determined to be optimistic about everything. "And you're getting along well with Lorenzo?"

I nodded. This was not the time to tell her how far apart we had grown. He spent very little time in Soledad, and I seldom visited him in Palma. He lied to me about his travels, too, for once when he told me

he had gone to Barcelona I found hotel receipts from
Tunisia and Tangier in his pocket. And then there
was the near accident on the road earlier that day. I
could not be certain the car that almost ran me down
was Lorenzo's Mercedes, but it was quite a coincidence that he had arrived at Soledad so shortly afterward.

I decided the best thing was to change the subject.
"Doña Catalina, just wait until you see Mimi! She's
grown so since she was here the last time. And she's
learning so much. Valerie is a marvelous teacher—
and she has such a way with children. I'm just delighted."

"You like her, don't you? And what a coincidence,
her coming from the place where you spent so much
time as a child!"

I had forgotten that I had written and told Doña
Catalina about our discovery. Now I was glad I had,
for it allowed me to talk about pleasant things. "Oh,
yes, it was such a delightful surprise." I chatted on,
talking mostly about my childhood and the happy
summers I had enjoyed in Connecticut. Eventually
we ran out of small talk, and we just sat together
quietly, comfortable in our affection for each other.
I could see that she had relaxed, for her breathing
seemed less labored.

Suddenly Doña Catalina rose. "I have something
here for your friend, since you like her so much. I've
had this shell for years. It comes from near Soledad,
as a matter of fact. If Valerie's interested in nature
she'll like this shell—it's very unusual."

Before I could interfere, Doña Catalina was across
the room, standing on tiptoe, stretching to reach
a shell on the top shelf of a cupboard. The next moment she was on the floor. The effort of moving and
the strain of reaching had brought on another attack.

The old lady's teeth were clenched with pain, and
her frail body shuddered as she struggled for breath.

Frantically I called for Conchita and together we managed to carry her to the bed. My eyes swiftly scanned the bedside table and dresser top, finally locating the bottle of medicine. Nitroglycerin: one tablet to be placed under the patient's tongue.

Conchita was standing uselessly by the bed, wringing her hands and moaning. "Snap out of it!" I commanded her sharply. "Help me to give Doña Catalina her medication." Carefully we pressed the unconscious woman's jaws to unlock her clenched teeth, and inserted the tablet as directed.

Within minutes Doña Catalina appeared to revive. Her color improved and the terrible tightness seemed to leave her chest. She coughed feebly and her head sank wearily on the pillow, but I knew the danger had passed. Our next step was to make her as comfortable as possible and find out how to ease her condition.

I looked up at Conchita. "We must get a doctor."

"He isn't here, he's on the mainland! Oh, what will we do?" Conchita was tearing at her hair in fright. "Poor Doña Catalina—what will happen to her? I told her she shouldn't stay here, sick as she is. I told her—"

I had had enough of the girl's hysterics. "That's enough! I'll go and get some help," I told her. "You stay here with Doña Catalina. She's had a severe shock and she must be terribly weak and frightened. I'll try to find a doctor—or get an ambulance to take her to Cuidadela," if necessary.

I left the house in search of a shop or a neighbor's house from which I could phone a doctor. The first building I passed was a small café that served the sailors who used the small harbor close to Doña Catalina's own dock. I hurried inside. There were two men standing near the small bar, and they looked up as I entered. I barely glanced at them. "May I use your phone?" I asked the proprietor.

"You will have to wait, *señora*. There is someone using it now, and these men are next in line. They want to call Majorca, and you know that takes time."

I turned to the two men. They were obviously travelers, for their faces were dark from the sun and they had the look of men who have been long at sea. One had thick red hair and a heavy beard. The other was bearded, too, but his hair was black. I judged him to be Spanish.

They seemed interested in my problem. The redhaired man spoke. "Trouble?"

"Oh, yes. I must find a doctor. My friend, Doña Catalina, is very ill. I must find out what we can do for her—she might have to go to the hospital. Please, may I use the phone before you? Time is passing, and I don't know how long she can go without attention."

The red-haired man stepped forward. "What's her trouble? I'm a physician. I'm not licensed to practice here, but I'm sure under the circumstances I can help."

I clutched his arm. "Across the road . . . please . . . oh, thank you. I never expected . . . ."

We virtually flew across the road to Doña Catalina's house. I led the way upstairs to her room, and smiled my reassurance to Conchita. "They're doctors. I'm sure they can help."

Conchita stepped aside to let them examine her mistress, who seemed to have lapsed into an exhausted sleep. The red-haired man looked at me inquiringly and then listened intently as I ran through a hurried account of what had happened. I finished by handing him the bottle of tablets.

"Oh," I told him, "it was such good luck I found you!" A calm seemed to have come over me in this young man's presence. "We really had quite a fright. Was it serious? Could it have been fatal?"

"Hard to say. Very possibly it could have been. Hasn't she a physician who attends her?"

I explained that her doctor had considered her out

of danger and had gone away for a few days. "What shall we do until he returns?"

"Plenty of rest. Quiet. She shouldn't even try to talk, though I expect she won't particularly want to right now." He glanced toward the bed. "She should be watched closely—the first few days after such an attack are the most critical period. Aren't there other doctors on Minorca?"

"Yes, in Cuidadela. But they probably won't come all the way over here unless it's a crisis." I looked directly at him. "Is it possible for you to stay—until her own physician returns?"

He glanced from me to Doña Catalina. Then he met his companion's questioning gaze. "Madam, my companion is professor Diego Sorlantes. We are staying on our boat, anchored in the cove nearby. I have some medicine there I'd like to give the *doña*—an injection to temporarily stabilize her condition."

"Oh, by all means send for it. Will you stay, then—both of you?"

He nodded. "Diego, bring my whole bag, if you will." His friend nodded and left the room. Conchita was sitting by the bed, considerably calmed herself by now, so I stepped aside. I would have to arrange a place for the two men to stay—and I would have to plan something to eat. In the excitement I was sure no one had thought about dinner.

I was wrong. The cook, like a proper servant obeying orders, had proceeded with the preparation of the evening meal. I glanced at my watch. Almost six. Valerie and Mimi would be along very soon.

When I returned to Doña Catalina's room, I had made the necessary preparations for houseguests. Valerie, Mimi and I would sleep in the room I generally used when I spent a few days with my elderly friend. A cot had been put in for Mimi, and the twin beds were made up.

The two men would stay in another room, closer

to Doña Catalina's chambers, so the doctor could tend to her if she woke and needed him. I had often been amused at the grand size of Doña Catalina's house. Now I was thankful that it had so many rooms.

Doña Catalina was awake when I returned. I hurried to her side. "My dear—" I spoke quietly, then realized it was not necessary to whisper "—you've had another attack, more severe than usual. I found a doctor at the café and he's taking care of you. He'll be staying until your own doctor returns."

She tried to speak, but the effort seemed too much for her. She gestured with her hand. "Oh." I was surprised at my ability to interpret her signals. "This is Professor Diego Sorlantes. And Dr.—" I realized for the first time that I didn't know the other man's name. I looked up at him questioningly.

"Dr. Mark Lefevre."

I felt a shock. Mark? Here? Then I remembered that Doña Catalina was waiting for me to continue. "Dr. Mark Lefevre." I repeated his name slowly. Doña Catalina closed her eyes. Already, she was exhausted.

I rose and looked at Mark's face. Was this really the boy I had known when I was young? Valerie's cousin? He looked so different. His beard . . . . He had never had a beard! I repeated his name, my voice rising as if I were asking a question. "Mark Lefevre?"

"At your service, ma'am." He bowed gallantly. "And to whom am I speaking?"

I still was too amazed to respond. I had not been prepared to see him. And now . . . . "Crystal Derbly." I realized what I had said. I had forgotten my married name. I stuttered, "No! Crystal Santos." I drew back, hoping he had not noticed my error—that he had not heard me say my maiden name.

"Crystal Derbly!" His eyes widened. "My little Crystal?"

I shook my head violently. "No!" I was trembling and I felt like a fool. "No, I'm Crystal Santos." I em-

phasized the last name. "I'm married to Lorenzo Santos—the art dealer."

He responded immediately to my confusion. Suddenly he was very formal, as if we were strangers
meeting for the first time. "Crystal Santos. Diego,
meet Mrs. Santos, the art dealer's wife."

Diego bowed. "Delighted to meet you. Mark told
me his cousin was working for you." He seemed not
at all surprised.

"Then you got her letter?" I felt the excitement.
Valerie had thought it had reached Mexico too late.

"Yes, just before we set sail. So we headed directly
for the Balearic Islands. I certainly never expected to
see you on Minorca." Mark was smiling delightedly.

I explained the purpose of our visit. "Valerie and
Mimi ought to be arriving any moment. Oh, Val will
be so happy to see you!"

His voice was low. "And you aren't?"

I blushed. Was I unhappy that we'd met, after all?
I couldn't pretend that I was. "Oh, no. I'm very pleased.
It's been a long time. So you're a doctor now!"

I knew I sounded silly—condescending. But I
couldn't help it. I dared not reveal my pleasure at
seeing Mark so unexpectedly. How could I know what
significance the youthful affection we'd shared held
for him now? I treasured my memories of Mark but
I could not tell whether he felt as I did.

"Yes." His voice sent a shiver of delight up my
spine. It was still the same—deep, resonant. But more
mature. He was not a youth any longer. And I was
not a young girl. We were adults. I shivered suddenly.
Adults—with adult emotions.

"Remember the time we tried to sail upriver in my
sailboat and grounded on a sandbar?" He was smiling
and relaxed, assuring me that he would respect the
boundaries I put on our friendship. "Remember how
scared you were?"

I laughed with relief. "Scared? I was terrified!" I

turned to Diego. "Did he ever tell you about that time? The beast really frightened me! He started talking about dry bones on desert sand, and how our bodies would be found—someday—by explorers. I was only about twelve, I guess, and he had me believing that we'd never get free—and we'd never be rescued. It was very cruel of him." I didn't sound as if I still believed he was cruel. I was laughing with pleasure at the memory.

Diego chuckled. "This character has told me almost everything that's ever happened to him. We spent a lot of days alone on the *Cris.* It's a long way here from Mexico."

Mark guffawed. "You think *you* were bored! You should try listening to a man tell you about all the marvelous twirls in snail shells. Honest, that's all he talks about—hour after hour. That's what I get for taking a sea voyage with a marine biologist!"

I joined in the laughter. It was clear that these two men were good friends.

I met Mark's eyes and knew I would be safe with him. He was willing to let me decide the level of intimacy our relationship could reach. We could be just good friends—if that was what I wished.

When Valerie and Mimi arrived, Mark threw his arms around his cousin's waist and lifted her up in his arms like a big playful dog who has found an old favorite toy. I watched in silence, barely able to conceal my envy. For one moment I let myself imagine his arms embracing me. Then with a shrug of my shoulders I pushed the thought aside. I could not indulge in such dreams. . . .

After a pleasant dinner, Valerie pulled out her wallet and presented Mark with a picture. "That's Soledad—where we're staying. Crystal inherited it from an aunt. Isn't it wonderful to have rich friends?" she laughed teasingly.

Mark took the picture and studied it in silence.

Then he held it out to me. "Which one of those men is your husband?"

I glanced at the picture. Valerie had taken it on the day Lorenzo arrived with her car, and I had promptly forgotten it. I pointed at Lorenzo, standing between me and Mimi.

Mark looked at the photograph again. "A handsome man . . . very distinguished. Are you happy with him?"

The question was so sudden, I was not prepared with a quick answer. But I forced myself to reply, "Yes. Very."

He did not respond. Instead he looked once more at the photo. "That other man—who is he?"

"Miguel." I was in control of my voice again. "Lorenzo's chauffeur."

"Miguel." He said the name slowly, as if trying to make it fit the image. "Funny, I have a feeling I've seen him somewhere before. Why can't I place him?" He held the picture out to Diego. "Doesn't he look familiar to you?"

Diego nodded. "A little. But we've met so many people, in so many places—it's hard to say for sure."

I could see that Mark was not satisfied. He turned back to me. "When Doña Catalina's physician returns, you'll be going back to Majorca, won't you?" I nodded. "Well, then, you'd better tell me now, so I can get accustomed to it. What shall I call you, when we meet your husband? Crystal? Or Mrs. Santos?"

I tried to decide, but I must have taken too long to answer. He nodded. "I can tell. Diego, meet Mrs. Santos! And remember: for some reason or another, it's important that we keep our distance. At least when Lorenzo is around." He turned back to me. "The jealous type, eh? Typical Spaniard."

I shook my head. Then abruptly I nodded. "Yes,

you're right. The jealous type." I knew suddenly that
it would be safer for Mark if he continued to believe
that Lorenzo was a suspicious man. It would keep
him on his guard.

Chapter 12

Don Cristobal Reyes arrived the following morning. I met him at the dock with the news of Doña Catalina's condition. "I hope you didn't have to leave any important appointments," I hurried on. "I just knew you'd want to be with your sister when she was so ill."

"You were absolutely right. Nothing is more important to me than my sister's health. I appreciate your phone call. And I'll have something to say to her doctor. What negligence! How could he be sure she wouldn't need him? Damn, he's responsible for her. Doesn't he know that?"

"I'm sure he does, Dr. Reyes. But you shouldn't blame him. He has other patients, too, and I'm sure he deserves some time off."

Dr. Reyes nodded. "You're right, of course. I just feel so frustrated. What if you hadn't come early? If she'd been alone with that empty-headed Conchita, she might have died. . . ."

Still, when he saw his sister, and spoke with Mark, he calmed down. It was obvious that Doña Catalina was much improved. As long as she had plenty of

rest and did not exert herself, she could lead a fairly
normal life.

Valerie, Mimi and I left for Majorca right after lunch.
Mark and Diego promised to come to Soledad soon—
after they had a chance to explore the caves and grottoes that abounded on Minorca, especially near the
city of Cuidadela.

When Dr. Reyes heard that Diego was a marine
biologist, he became very animated. "Oh, you'll find
Soledad an absolute delight. There's a grotto just offshore from the main estate where very rare algae
grows. You must see it—and collect some for your
laboratory. I understand the species is unique to this
part of the world."

Diego could not contain his eagerness. "And you
said you didn't think we ought to go there at all!"
Though he spoke to Mark I could not help but hear
what he said.

"Not come to Soledad? Why, Mark, how could you?
We have plenty of room—and you're more than welcome. I'd be very disappointed if you didn't stay for
at least a while."

"And Lorenzo? What will he feel about it?"

I shook my head. "Please, don't make decisions for
me. Soledad is my home—mine! I invite any guests
I choose. So many of the people I met over the years
when father was alive and working in the foreign
service have dropped by. I've made it clear that my
house is open to my friends."

He looked at me without smiling. "And Lorenzo?
You still haven't told me what he'd think."

"Why, nothing. You have to understand—Lorenzo
and I feel differently about entertaining. He wines
and dines his clients when he's in Palma, because
they're important to his business. But otherwise he
doesn't care for parties, big or small." I paused, remembering his intimate little "party" with Dolores,
Miguel and Peraldez. Then I continued. "So I have

them at Soledad—usually when Lorenzo is in town
or on a business trip. He knows about my guests; I
don't try to keep my friends from him. But he honestly
prefers not to be involved. Besides, he's very busy."

I hoped my explanation would satisfy Mark, and
it seemed to do so. We were almost at the dock. Soon
we would say our farewells and be on our way.

Diego fell in beside Dr. Reyes. "Did you know that
Mark and Valerie and Crystal grew up together in the
United States? In Connecticut. Quite a coincidence,
isn't it?"

Mark laughed. "Ah, yes. The three of us made mud
pies together in the sand!"

Dr. Reyes chuckled. "Quite an achievement in itself! But surely you found other, more interesting
things to do when you grew up?"

I spoke quickly. "Well, maybe we made sand castles
then. But it doesn't matter. Sand castles get washed
away by the tide."

I caught Mark's eyes and then looked away. He
was studying me very solemnly. As we approached
the shore he pulled me to one side. "Are you certain
we won't cause trouble if we stay at Soledad? If
you were my wife, I'm not sure I'd want you to frat-
ernize with old boyfriends."

I tried to ignore the implications of his words. Did
he really consider himself an old boyfriend? And as
such, would he upset Lorenzo? Then I remembered
how uninterested Lorenzo was in my life. If he hadn't
already tried to kill me, he at least wanted me out of
the way. Mark's presence at Soledad might add to
my safety.

"I'm sure you'll be welcome—by Lorenzo as well
as by me. Please, don't hesitate to come as soon as
you can. We'd . . . Val would be very disappointed
if you didn't."

"All right. We'll be there. But Cris—" he looked
straight into my eyes "—believe me when I say I want

you to be happy. I don't want to do anything to spoil your life here."

"Don't worry, you won't. And thanks. It's nice to know you're still my friend after all these years." I felt safer. It was best that Mark not know I remembered we'd ever been anything more.

On the way across to Soledad, Mimi had a chance to show Valerie the flying fish. Then, delighted at the number, she occupied herself with counting them. Val turned to me. It was the first private moment we'd had in days. "I can't get used to Mark in that beard," she commented. "I think he looks terrible!"

I couldn't agree with her. "Well, it was a surprise. I honestly didn't recognize him at first." I forced a laugh. "Maybe he grew it to please a woman in Mexico."

"If he did, she's going to get pretty lonesome. He told me he and Diego planned to be gone for six months."

"Maybe. But I think the loneliest people are those who have nothing—and nobody—to wait for."

Valerie was silent for a moment. When she spoke again, she had dismissed her cousin from her thoughts. "Crystal, I think Patrick ought to be back soon. He said he'd be gone only a few weeks. There should be some news from him by now."

"I hope so." I felt the weight returning. We were coming close to land. "What did you say to Mark about him?"

"Not much—just that he and Lorenzo had had a disagreement over the value of a painting he did. I told him it would be a good idea if he didn't mention Patrick to Lorenzo."

"How soon will Mark and Diego leave Cuidadela?"

"Pretty soon. But they might not come directly to Soledad. They want to explore the entire archipelago: Ibiza, Formentera, even little Cabrera. I didn't press them for details. They didn't seem too sure of their plans."

I pulled the boat into the slip. Miguel had seen us approach, and he caught the rope and tied it to the post. We could not continue our conversation. I did not want Miguel to know in advance that friends were coming. I wished to keep Mark and Diego away from the danger that he—that all of Soledad—now seemed to represent.

THE NEXT DAY LORENZO and Miguel returned to Palma. I felt relieved to see them go and in my elation insisted that Val and I drive together into Pollensa to get the mail. But there was no letter from Patrick in her box, as she had expected. She turned away, disappointed.

The postal employee was new, and seemed to feel personally responsible for her unhappiness. He fussed for a moment among the boxes, and then suddenly his face lighted up. "Oh, *señorita! Un momento.* I haven't looked in the other box."

I turned, surprised. "The other box? There is no other box. I was here when my husband rented this one for us."

"I don't know, *señora.* But I do know there is a second box. We have been informed that mail for Miss Roberts is to go into that box, along with special letters for Señor Santos. Then he or his chauffeur picks it all up. But I'm sure it will be all right to give it to you." He pulled a handful of letters from a box some distance removed from the one I knew.

I took it silently and thumbed through the pieces. Most were directed to Lorenzo, and I handed them back. But a letter from Patrick was among them, and I gave it to Valerie. She opened it quickly. I waited while she read it in silence.

At last she looked up. "He's coming back. Soon. Maybe this week. Oh, Crystal! Isn't it wonderful?"

"In a way." I was still disturbed by my discovery.

I knew now why I had not received any of Patrick's letters in the few weeks before my breakdown. "It might cause a lot of trouble—for us all."

"You don't want him to come?"

"Of course I do! But it will bring things to a head." I wondered if Patrick's arrival would increase my danger. Would his life be threatened, too? I led the way back to the car. "Valerie, is it all right if I drop you back at Soledad? I want to go in to Palma for a while."

"Why, of course." Valerie climbed into the car. "You don't want me to come with you, do you?"

"No, thanks. I have to talk to Lorenzo." I gave no further explanation, nor did Val ask for one. She clutched the letter to her breast as we drove toward Soledad, and I knew she was thinking of Patrick and of how happy she was that he would soon be home again.

Lorenzo answered the phone at the town house when I called from the outskirts of Palma. He was surprised I had followed him, but he did not seem displeased. He was waiting downstairs when I arrived. My heart was pounding. "I told Valerie I had some business to do in town." I wanted him to know that someone knew where I was. If anything happened to me . . . .

He seemed unperturbed. "Fine. What is it, Crystal? I don't have a lot of time right now. I have an appointment at the gallery in an hour."

I nodded. "I just wanted to tell you. Dr. Reyes met us in Minorca and told me that Patrick was coming back. I think you ought to know."

He had been sitting beside me, but now he leaped to his feet. "Patrick? Coming back to Majorca? Is he crazy? What good does he expect to do here? Hasn't he caused enough trouble? I suppose Don Cristobal has his reasons for being friendly to a thief, but—"

I interrupted him with a voice so calm I surprised

myself. "Please, Lorenzo. Don Cristobal knows everything. I spoke with him about it many times. He agrees with me that Patrick must get this all straightened out. If he doesn't, it will ruin his career."

"His career!" Lorenzo was almost apoplectic. "How dare he! What about my gallery? He could ruin me! If I hadn't been able to placate Peraldez . . . ." He clenched his fists. "God knows what might have happened!"

I remembered again the four of them at the little private gathering, drinking and singing together. How, I wondered, could Lorenzo speak of Peraldez as if he were an enemy when they were such good friends? What kind of bond existed between them?

Lorenzo was too excited to notice my expression. He swung his fist and slammed it against the back of a chair. "If Patrick dares to set foot here again, or does anything to stir up a scandal, I'll have him run off the island. And I warn you, Crystal—"

"Warn me?" I stood to face him. I was angry, too. He glared at me for a moment, and then he turned away. I stood my ground. "Lorenzo, I want this clear between us. Patrick is my brother. Unless you permit him to turn the entire affair over to the police so he can be proven innocent—or guilty—I will continue to allow him to visit Soledad. It is my house! And as for your precious scandal . . . you seem to have taken care of it. I'll tell you right now, Dr. Reyes was shocked when I told him you wouldn't call the police."

He paced nervously, but he didn't interrupt me. So I continued. "If the neighbors wonder about anything, it might be at how often we are apart—and how seldom my brother comes to visit us here, in your home. I honestly feel like a stranger in this place!" I was warming up. "And as for your running Patrick off the island, I don't think you can do it. You have a lot of friends—but so do I."

He was still pacing, and I felt the need to placate

him. "I honestly think the Picasso will turn up sooner or later."

Lorenzo snickered. "You do, do you? Well, you ought to know, since your brother is the one who has it. Unless he sold it when he was in England. Yes, I know he was there. And I know he was on the island just a few weeks ago. Crystal, your petty female intrigues are so transparent!"

He turned toward me, and suddenly I was caught in his arms. "Crystal, don't you realize I've been trying to protect you? Can't you see that your brother is a money-hungry, spoiled child who saw you suddenly become a very wealthy woman? Don't you understand that he is jealous because Soledad was left to you? He wants it—and he wants me out of the way."

I forced myself to resist his touch. He couldn't win me in this way—not anymore. "Lorenzo, please. Patrick must be given a chance to clear his name. He's innocent—I know it. And I think you do, too. And if he isn't . . . then I'll admit you're right, and send him away for keeps." I was glad my voice remained steady. "But let me say it again. I don't think he's stolen anything. I'm sure he's innocent."

Lorenzo's hands dropped to his sides and he walked away from me. When he spoke I knew he was angry once more. "You and your brother are both crazy. Lunatics! He thinks I'm fool enough to go along with his lies—and you . . . . You can't see how no-good he is!" He clenched his fists. "I forbid you to see him!"

I knew I was risking my own safety, but I was too angry to control myself. "I hear you, Lorenzo, but I refuse to obey. I'm sure the Picasso will be found. It won't be allowed to rot forever where it is hidden."

For a moment Lorenzo was silent. Then he began to laugh. A light, unexpected, unreal laugh. It was intolerable. I could endure it far less than I could endure his anger. He looked at me with a sudden

show of sympathy. "Oh, my poor Crystal. Your mind
is going again, isn't it? You're mixing dream with
reality. I think you'd better go back to Soledad. I don't
want you to break while you're here. My clients would
be upset if I presented them to an insane woman."
He shouted suddenly. "Miguel!"

Miguel appeared at the door. "Si, *señor*?"

"Get out the Mercedes and park madam's car in
the garage. I want you to drive Mrs. Santos back to
Soledad."

I began to protest. I could drive myself. I would not
let Lorenzo control me as he had done before. And
to my surprise, he agreed to let me go. "Just be careful."
His warning rang hollow. "I don't want you driving
off a cliff."

Clutching my keys, I ran to the street. The car
started easily and I was on my way. I did not think
just then how odd it was for Lorenzo to show such
concern after we had argued. And why had he given
in so easily when I insisted on driving home by myself?

The car responded quickly to my touch, and the
purr of the engine reassured me. I was being para-
noid. We had had a fight and I had won. I ought to
be pleased, not upset. And I had cleared the way for
Patrick to stay in my own house—where he belonged.
I smiled. How nice it would be for him not to have
to hide anymore. . . .

I reached the coastal road in record time, for I was
driving much faster than normal. Ahead was a long
slope that led to the cliff. Automatically, I touched
the brake.

Nothing happened. The car continued to move just
as swiftly. I pressed harder on the brake. Still I continued to speed down toward the sharp turn ahead.

I felt the sweat form on my brow, and on the palms
of my hands. I knew what had happened. Lorenzo
had tricked me into insisting that I drive my own car.

And he had had Miguel fix the brakes while we were quarreling. I would go over the cliff. And when my body was found, my death would be explained as an accident. I was certain that at least some of our neighbors had seen me rush out and drive away. Lorenzo would be pitied—and he would have what he wanted.

I tried to close my eyes to shut out the approaching moment of terror when the car would fly out over the water. But I could not shut them. I stared ahead, too frightened to scream. And the car rolled on, going faster with each passing minute.

Suddenly I recovered my senses and frantically turned the wheel. If I was lucky, I might end up in the dense brush that lined the side of the road back from the cliff. If I was lucky. . . . I turned slowly— steadily. And I prayed. And then, unable to contain my fright any longer, I screamed.

Chapter 13

The screams rang in my ears, and I wondered who was making such noise. My throat ached; my back was sore. I was the one who was screaming! I was shaking terribly, as if I had no control over my actions. Had I broken at last? Was this the final straw that would put me back where Lorenzo wanted me—not in the clinic again, but in an asylum?

I felt suddenly calm. It hadn't worked. He had tried to kill me—and he had failed. I was alive!

But was I injured? I felt my arms, my ribs. Carefully, I moved my legs. Nothing seemed broken. And the car? I climbed out cautiously. My attempt to save myself had succeeded only because the road turned so gradually and I had made a sharp turn to the right—away from the ocean. The thick brush had done the rest of the work. It had grabbed at the car and dragged me to a stop.

The front grille of the car looked somewhat battered and there were deep scratches along the sides, but otherwise little damage was apparent. I had cut a swath through the brush that I could use in backing up. That is, if I wanted to use my car again. If I dared. The brakes were no good, that I knew. However, I could still drive safely—if I went slowly. I stood undecided for a moment, testing inner strength. Did I have the courage to start the car again? Or should I walk?

It was far to Soledad. The road was deserted and the sun shone hotly. In my anxiety to be back safely with those whom I loved and trusted, I felt it was worth the risk to try the car once more.

I had turned off the engine when I aimed toward the brush. Now I had to try to start it again. If I failed . . . . I decided not to think too far ahead. One step at a time. I climbed in and turned the key in the ignition.

The engine roared into life. With a feeling of great relief I backed slowly onto the highway and shifted cautiously into forward gear. The car began to move ahead. Knowing the danger I faced, I did not shift into a high gear. Instead I kept it in first, barely creeping along the road. I had no fear that I would have trouble stopping again. At the slow speed I was traveling, just running off the road would bring the car to a halt.

When the road left the cliffs I dared to increase my speed, but it still seemed to take hours for me to cover the distance to safety. I reached Soledad just as Eulalia was gathering vegetables from the kitchen garden for the evening meal. She ran to my side as I practically staggered from the car.

I spent most of that day in bed, resting from the strain and deciding my best course of action. There seemed no point in going to the police about the incident. Although I had no doubt the brakes had been tampered with, I somehow knew they would be reluctant to accept my story. After all, I was the wife of the highly respected Señor Santos—a woman, moreover, who had recently suffered a nervous breakdown. Lorenzo would certainly not hesitate to bring up the scandal of the missing Picasso, implicating Pat-

rick, if it were a question of his credibility over mine.
Most important, any such action on my part would
alert him to my suspicions, and I dared not think of
what might happen then. No, my best course seemed
to be to watch . . . and wait.

It was late in the afternoon when I went to the
beach with Valerie and Mimi. They cavorted like two
dolphins, rushing into the waves and leaping up,
shouting with glee when the water splashed over
them. I had no heart for such play. I had not told
anyone of my suspicion that the car's sudden brake
failure had been no accident. Valerie, unaware of the
care I customarily gave my car, accepted what had
happened. Her brakes had gone bad—why couldn't
mine?

It did me good to see others behaving in a normal
manner. My inclination was to crawl into my room
and never leave it. To secure my safety by hiding. But
watching Valerie, I knew such a ploy would not work.
It would not be enough for me to be safe because I
was afraid to move. Like Patrick, who was determined
to get to the bottom of his problem, to find the Picasso
and prove his innocence, I had to learn why I was so
great a threat to Lorenzo that he felt he had to destroy
me.

Was it something I knew—or that he thought I
knew—that might interfere with what he was doing?
I explored that idea very thoroughly and finally tossed
it aside. As far as I could see, he was doing nothing
illegal. Except trying to kill me. But his business was
perfectly legitimate. I had witnessed many of his sales
and they were proper in every way. Oh, he charged
high prices for his goods, but he dealt in valuable
objets d'art. In some cases he actually took less for
his pieces than was standard market price.

Nor did he try to substitute less valuable pieces for
the ones purchased when he delivered them. In fact,
his deliveries were very aboveboard, often being made

by friends who happened to be traveling from Majorca to wherever the customer lived. Many times, my friends—often active in diplomatic affairs—served as deliverymen for Lorenzo. It was a practice I did not totally condone, but I couldn't find anything illegal about it. In fact, as Lorenzo had told me many times, that method of delivery guaranteed safe arrival of the purchase. Many commercial delivery firms were careless with their cargo.

If not his business, then what terrible secret was it that he feared I might have knowledge of? I could think of nothing. And so, at last, I had to face the fact more frightening to me—that he had married me for Soledad, and that he wanted to get rid of me now so he could marry Dolores, the only woman he truly loved.

What terrified me the most was the realization that in both attempts on my life there had been an element of accident. Surely I could not prove that a car had deliberately tried to run me down on the road that day before we left for Minorca. Few people used the road for walking, and a driver had no reason to expect a pedestrian just around a curve. As for the brakes— could I prove they had been tampered with? I knew I could not. When I later delivered the car to the garage in Pollensa, the repair mechanic informed me that the brake lines had both somehow developed a leak. An unusual occurrence, he said, but not impossible. I was one lucky lady. . . .

THREE DAYS AFTER my terrible experience, Mark and Diego appeared suddenly at our dock. They called out as they slid in to anchor, and as soon as their boat was moored, leaped overboard and swam to where we sat on the beach.

I had been sitting near the shore, combing out the tangles in my hair and listening to Mimi and Valerie at play. Mark waded up beside me. Feeling his intent

gaze upon me, I averted my eyes, reluctant for him
to view there the pleasure I felt at his arrival. "Remember how I used to say you reminded me of the
little mermaid in the port of Copenhagen?" he greeted
me.

I was not prepared for his casual resumption of
conversation—as if we had not been apart for more
than two weeks. "I didn't expect you. Don't you believe in writing?"

"Not when I'm as close as we are." I wasn't sure
how he meant that, so I let it pass. "So you don't
remember? Well, maybe it meant more to me. I can
see that you're happy as you are, and for that I'm
glad. It's a bit easier to get adjusted to your being
married, now that I can see you are content."

Still I did not look up at him. He laughed. "Aren't
you glad we came? At least Valerie said hello. You
won't even look at me!"

I turned my head—and found myself face-to-face
with a memory. "You've shaved your beard off!"

"Do you mind if I sit down? Yes, it's gone. Oh, I
saw the look on your face—and on Val's. Neither of
you liked it. And to be honest, neither did I. But on
the voyage it was just too much trouble to shave every
day. I feel younger without it. Do I look better?"

I could not take my eyes from his face. He was the
same, after all! The same strong jaw, the same con-
toured cheeks. The same green eyes under straight
brows. The same sparkle in the eyes that had charmed
me when I was eighteen.

He hadn't changed much physically, either. His
body was firm and muscular—a solid figure of a man.
He seemed stronger than Lorenzo. Not so delicate in
the hips, and with firm biceps. There was a calmness
about him—a security. I wanted to crawl into his arms
and beg for protection.

Yet I knew that was the one thing I dared not do.
It was important that he believe I was happy with

Lorenzo. The love that might exist between us was impossible. I was married to Lorenzo. And Mark must not be drawn into my problems.

I decided right then on the best approach. "You're quite a good-looking guy! You must let me introduce you to some of my neighbors and show you off to the tourists. You could make a lot of women happy—if you wanted to."

A shadow crossed his face, and I wondered painfully if I had offended him. Then he laughed. "Come on, now, you're not playing fair. I'm here for a rest! Oh, Diego thinks I'm hot to find algae—but I don't care about it at all. And as for women . . . ." He shrugged his shoulders. "I have enough of them in Mexico. I don't want any more complications in my life."

I took his cue. "Tell me about Mexico, Mark. Is it very different from here? Or Connecticut?"

"Very different—from both places. But I like it. I work in a large hospital where we treat mostly the very poor. And oh, Crystal, there are so many of them! The children are the most pathetic. And yet the country has a decent health system. Even the dump dwellers can get medical aid if they need it."

"Dump dwellers?"

"Yes. Believe it or not, people live right on top of the city dump. Over garbage! They graze their sheep on trash, and they hunt through the dump for repairable objects they can fix up and sell. It's horrible . . . but for them it's a way of life." He went on then, talking about Mexico—its strange mixture of great beauty and terrible squalor; of ancient historic sites and the most modern architecture in the world.

And then, without realizing it, we slipped into a game of "remember when?" "Do you remember when my mast broke? And the day the eel bit you? The time we went fishing with the luring lights—and our par ents caught us and threatened to call the coast guard to teach us a lesson?"

I laughed at each memory as he brought it back. "Remember the old woman we were certain was a witch?" I had my share of memories, too, and now they flooded back.

"Oh, yes!" He chuckled. "And the fat girl we scared with crabs? You know, she grew up to be a very beautiful woman. Tell me, Cris, why didn't you come back to Old Saybrook?"

"Well, mother died while I was in college—and I guess it was too painful for dad to return to where we had all had so much fun."

Diego, Valerie and Mimi were coming toward us. Val ran up and threw her arms around Mark. "Oh, you look wonderful without all that hair! I'm so glad you came. But I hardly knew you from a distance; I thought it was some stranger come to court Crystal."

"A few years too late, I'm afraid." Mark had risen as they approached, and he looked down at me. "Did you meet Lorenzo here? It must have been about the time you inherited this place. It's really magnificent—at least what I can see from the beach. And those three boats are all yours? Well, I may be jealous, but I can't deny that Majorca has been good to you."

I did not meet his eyes. "Yes, it did happen that way—but not quite. First I inherited Soledad. Then I met Lorenzo. I might even say I met him *because* of Soledad."

"Because of Soledad?" Valerie looked surprised. "I got the idea he didn't like the place very much. . . ."

"Oh, he does like it. He gets out here as often as he can, considering how busy he is. And he loves to go boating—especially in the yacht."

"Yes, I've noticed that. When he is here, he's usually out at sea with Miguel." Valerie seemed to object to his neglect of me.

I rushed to my husband's defense. "Well, you can't

blame him. He works very hard and he needs to relax."

"Of course. I didn't mean it as a criticism. Go on," she encouraged me. "I'm interested in hearing more about you two."

"Well, long before I inherited Soledad, Lorenzo bought the Casa Juarez, in Palma. When he found out that Soledad had at one time been owned by the same Juarez family, he decided he'd like to restore the property to one owner. He had his lawyer contact Aunt Melina—but she wouldn't even talk to him. Neither would I, when I inherited the property. I fell in love with it on first sight."

"Anyone would." Valerie looked at her cousin. "It's so beautiful!"

"Then, one morning when I got back from sailing, I noticed an unfamiliar motorboat tied to the dock in the cove. A few minutes later, a frogman surfaced with a load of bottles."

"Bottles?" Mark had not expected that, I could see.

"Yes. The cove is very deep, and there have been shipwrecks here in the past. And I suppose people have thrown things into the water, too. Anyway, some of the bottles were very old—and valuable. Lorenzo was exploring the caves underwater. He asked my permission to return." Somehow, I did not want to remember his courtship. "Three months later we were married."

"Before he moved to Palma, where did Lorenzo live?" It seemed a natural question for Mark to ask.

"In Barcelona."

"Did he always live there?"

"No, only since . . . ." I paused. "I really can't say. He's a native of southern Spain. To tell you the truth, we haven't talked a lot about what happened before we met."

"I'm sorry, I didn't mean to pry." Then he looked down at Mimi. "My, you look just like your mother did when she was your age! Did I tell you that the first time we met?"

Mimi was flattered by his attention. She smirked and fluttered her eyelids. We all broke into laughter.

Mark turned back to me. "Cris, I hope you don't mind our taking you up on your invitation." He hurried on, "We'll be staying on board ship, but if we could anchor in the cove for a few days . . . ."

"Oh, certainly! And you must come to dinner tonight. Lorenzo will be back from Palma—and I'll invite Dr. Reyes. Lorenzo will be delighted to meet you." I wasn't sure he would be, but I hoped his natural good manners would conceal any irritation he might feel upon finding company at Soledad. It would be the first time he had seen me since my near accident. I wondered if he would be able to conceal his disappointment that I was alive and uninjured. And not mentally upset. . . .

In the days since my terrible experience on the cliff, I had come to doubt my first fears. I could find no real reason for Lorenzo to want me dead—except the possibility that he might want to marry Dolores. But he had known her for years before he met me. If he had wanted to marry her, he had had many opportunities.

So I was considering the possibility that maybe, after all, the brake lines had been damaged accidentally. Still, I appreciated the presence of company on our first meeting. If I was wrong . . . . I just did not want to be alone with Lorenzo. At least not right away. I followed Mark and Valerie up the path to the house. Mark was asking Val to visit her father, and she did not seem pleased at the prospect, even when he assured her that she was missed by both her father and her stepmother.

Lorenzo arrived at Soledad just in time to sit down for dinner. I was delighted by his behavior. He was the perfect host—charming, courteous, totally captivating. If Mark had had any doubts that I was happily married, Lorenzo allayed his fears. We made a perfect picture, sitting at either end of the table, smiling at each other. And when the dinner was over he sat next to me on a bench in the garden as we all discussed the beauty of Majorca and the pleasures of boating.

Mark and Diego, whom we dubbed "the Mexicans," visited Soledad often after that night. Lorenzo took them aboard the yacht to visit the island of Cabrera. He organized a climb of Puig Major, the highest mountain on the islands. He even suggested and arranged for a visit to Valdemosa, where the souvenirs of George Sand and Chopin are enshrined. We all went along, and I could see that Diego was very impressed by the story of the two most famous French artists of Majorca.

"It's too bad you didn't own Soledad when they were alive; you'd have made them welcome. Imagine them having to go to a convent for shelter! It's outrageous how people treat artists just because they are different."

I thought of Patrick and I sighed. He was not being treated well, either. I expected him any day—and I was beginning to worry at the delay. Had he run into some trouble? I had grown so comfortable with Mark and Diego that I hoped they would meet my brother. For Mark and Patrick it would be a reunion, possibly as pleasant as Mark's and mine had been. Another chance to play "remember when?"

Mark did seem to have a calming influence on everyone. Lorenzo and I didn't fight when he was around, and even Dolores came out to Soledad to meet him. She spent four days with us, following a grand tour of the gallery that she provided for our guests.

I did not feel comfortable during her visit, for Lorenzo seemed to pay a great deal of attention to her. I was not exactly jealous; rather, their intimacy aroused in me all the suspicions and fears that I managed to forget while Lorenzo was so agreeable. Could I trust my husband, I asked myself constantly. If I judged him by his behavior when Mark was around, I most certainly could. Had he tried to kill me? It didn't seem possible. He was so attentive and kind to me. My confusion grew, and with it my confidence began to fail. Was I only imagining all my troubles?

My doubts were intensified on the afternoon of the third day of Dolores's stay. She had been growing increasingly restless, and at last she settled into a dark mood that no one could penetrate. Finally, Lorenzo took her inside the house. When they returned, Dolores was again in a bright, happy mood. What else could I believe but that Dolores was in love with Lorenzo, and they had been together—intimately?

I glanced quickly at Mark, but he seemed totally unaware of the time that had passed. I was ready to speak of my suspicions when Mark stepped to her side. "Dolores! I'm glad you're feeling better." He smiled comfortably. "I was thinking . . . how would you like to come to Ibiza with us? Diego and I would appreciate your company, and it would be very helpful to have someone with us who is knowledgeable about art. I understand there are many valuable, ancient pieces on display there. And I must confess, I'm a total ignoramus when it comes to telling one piece from another."

Lorenzo didn't react at all, and Dolores was obviously flattered. "You overestimate my qualities, Dr. Lefevre. I sincerely wish I could join you. However, I have my duties. I must tend the gallery." She cast a sidelong glance at Lorenzo. "This is our busiest time of year. Important customers arrive every day. Believe me, I would love to take the trip, but . . . ." She shrugged, then added, "And your boat is so interesting. To think you sailed all the way across the ocean in it! What is her name?"

"*Cris.*" Mark said the name swiftly, as if he wished to change the subject.

"*Cris.* An interesting name." Dolores seemed determined to force the issue. "Does it have any special meaning?" I felt certain she glanced sharply in my direction.

"No." I spoke up hurriedly. "It's just short for Criscraft. His first boat was made by them."

"Yes, that's it. By the way, Crystal, this one is a Criscraft, too, so you see I haven't changed my loyalties."

Lorenzo seemed unconcerned with the byplay. He stirred his drink absentmindedly and then suddenly suggested, "Why don't you take Crystal and Mimi with you? My wife knows the treasures of Ibiza very well."

I dared not answer, even when Mark, Diego and Valerie chattered gaily in anticipation of the week's outing. Lorenzo was planning something, of that I was sure. It was not like him to generously offer my company to another man—even in a closely chaperoned situation.

What was Lorenzo's game? Was he planning to trap me in a compromising position, so he would have an excuse for getting rid of me? That didn't seem likely, but I couldn't tell. Nor could I back out of the trip, for I would be disappointing four other people.

Once more I felt things closing in around me. And I knew I could do nothing to protect myself without letting Lorenzo know that I was aware of the danger I was in. Somehow I felt certain that security lay in my continued innocence. I had to play the game, too. If I slipped up, if I let on that I suspected Lorenzo of foul play, the game would end—and I would die.

But I could do what he suggested. If I were careful, I might find a way out—by learning what it was he really wanted. I was playing a difficult game; one with rules I did not understand. But it was worth the try.

Chapter 14

Patrick returned to Majorca the day Diego, Valerie, Mark, Mimi and I got back from the trip to Ibiza. True to my threat to Lorenzo, I established him in Soledad—an honored guest. Mark stayed on, too. Diego Sorlantes was far too interested in searching for new forms of algae to remain long in one spot, so he took the *Cris* and sailed off alone. I had already decided not to tell Patrick about Lorenzo's gathering at which Peraldez had been present, for I knew it would only anger him—and send him off on his pursuit of justice. And as long as Mark was visiting, I wanted to maintain the pretense of harmony in my family.

So the four of us hiked the hills around Soledad, gathering wild flowers, climbing up dry riverbeds, following ravines to their ends and pulling ourselves up the steep walls to look over on other, greener valleys. Mark was surprised at the acres of uncultivated land in my possession. I explained that Lorenzo had planned to terrace the land, but that he had become so busy at the gallery he had had no time to begin.

Mark shrugged. He commented that it must take

a great deal of money to run Soledad, and to keep Casa Juarez staffed and in repair.

Diego had arrived unexpectedly that morning, and he was with us as we hiked up the hillside. He chuckled. "You don't have to worry about your little Crystal's future. She's got a husband who's rolling in money!"

Both Mark and I looked at him in surprise. As far as we knew, he had last seen Lorenzo before he left on his most recent trip.

Diego continued, "Yeah! I ran into him in a casino in Monte Carlo. Well, that isn't quite correct. He didn't see me. But I sure saw him! He was playing roulette, and he was losing. I'll tell you, I never saw a man take such losses so casually. Any man who treats gambling losses that cavalierly has got to be loaded with money. . . ."

Patrick approached as Diego finished talking. "Lorenzo, a gambler? Crystal, did you know that?"

I shook my head. This was the second talent—or maybe interest—Lorenzo had of which I had been unaware. His singing and guitar playing—and now gambling! If I knew more about him, I felt certain I would be better able to handle myself in this difficult situation. Why, I wondered, had I never asked enough questions? Why had I just accepted him at face value?

"Well, he's got to have a big personal fortune to carry losses at gambling. His gallery isn't that profitable. I know—remember, I worked there for a while."

I had no response. I really didn't know what kind of money Lorenzo had. Our marriage contract had called for separation of property, rather common in marriages these days, so there had been no need for inventories of our personal assets. I shrugged the entire matter off with a flip remark about "making it big without even trying." Fortunately, no one seemed to want to continue discussing Lorenzo, so the subject was dropped.

Patrick hurried ahead. He had suggested that we visit the old farm where he had first met Valerie after they both arrived on Majorca. I suspected it was a nostalgic journey for the two of them. For me it was pure pleasure. Good company, good exercise—and release from the worries that always plagued me when I was alone.

As Mark, Diego and I approached the run-down farmhouse, we realized that Patrick and Valerie were still outside. Patrick turned to me. "Crystal? Do you know anything about this? The lock's been changed!" He stepped back and studied the building. "Well, I guess I'll have to try the chimney. I don't feel much like Santa Claus, but I do need my brushes and canvases." He moved to a low-hanging eave.

"Be careful!" I reached out a hand to stop him, but I was too slow. He was up on the roof and walking cautiously toward the chimney. He disappeared into the squat opening and we heard a terrible scuffle. Then, grumbling about the soot—and looking like a blackfaced comedian—he appeared at the window. "Crystal? Something odd is going on here. Do you know who's been doing all the diving since we were here last? Look. There are wet suits, tanks, flippers—enough for at least a dozen people!"

"Any guns or cameras?" Mark was chuckling. "Looks like we've found the stash of some second-story men!"

"No!" Patrick opened the window so we could look in. "Look for yourselves. Just diving equipment. Has Lorenzo been up here? He loves to dive."

"Sure he does. But he keeps his equipment on the yacht."

Mark took the easel and brushes that Patrick handed out. Then he assisted in removing the few canvases. "Is this all there is to the old farm?"

Patrick climbed out through the window and pulled it shut behind him. "I hope whoever put this stuff here doesn't notice that I've been inside. I don't want to cause any trouble."

I met his gaze. "You think it belongs to Lorenzo, don't you? But I'm sure you're wrong. Maybe he's letting a friend store these things here for a while."

"Yes, you're probably right." Patrick turned to Mark. "In answer to your question—no. There's an old stone tower over to the left a ways. It's a lot older than this building—and in much better repair. This place is going to fall down in the next heavy wind. The tower will be here forever." He started down the hill toward the house. "Let's go! I feel as if I'm crawling with spiders."

"Wait!" Mark was heading toward the tower. "What is this? The ruins of an old fortress?"

"Nothing quite so romantic," I explained. "It's an old watchtower built by the Moors to serve as a lookout for pirates. The big Moorish palaces were always built in the valleys. There are a lot of watchtowers all over the islands. They're wide on the top to allow space for the signal fires that were used to warn of danger approaching by sea. We use them to send neighborhood signals. Only we don't set fires, just hoist flags when we're home and receiving guests. Usually when Lorenzo and I are here we put one up." I glanced at the top of the tower. "Well! It's gone!"

Valerie spoke without thinking. "I heard Miguel say he'd take it down. I guess he did it because Mr. Santos went back to Palma."

She seemed to realize how odd that was even as she spoke. I was still at home. And I was the one who enjoyed visitors. Did Lorenzo disapprove of my having company? Did he intend Soledad to become a place of unhappy solitude for me? I did not pursue the matter right then, but resolved to speak to Lorenzo about it as soon as possible.

My thoughts were interrupted by the antics of Patrick, who had taken Valerie's hand and, whooping like a child, now raced with her down the hill toward the beach. Mark and Diego each grabbed one of my hands—but we descended a bit less precipitously. Diego was the first to speak. "I get the impression we're going to have a special treat, Mark. I understand Majorcan weddings are quite spectacular."

Mark chuckled. "No wonder Val was restless when we went to Ibiza. She was expecting Patrick to come back, wasn't she?"

I nodded. Yet I could not share Mark's optimistic assumption that Val and Patrick would soon be getting married. As long as the theft of the Picasso hung over my brother, I knew he would not feel free to marry Val, no matter how much they cared for each other.

Mark misinterpreted my silence. "Don't worry about my cousin. She's really a levelheaded kid. Oh, I know she has this crazy idea that her stepmother is a monster, but I think she'll get over that when she's no longer so dependent on her dad."

"What makes you so sure? She could have genuine reason to dislike her stepmother. Aren't you perhaps just taking a male point of view—assuming Val suffers from typical female jealousy?"

"Maybe. But I'm being objective, too. Val's mother died when Val was still young—and my uncle was still a young man himself. But from the very beginning Val refused to share him with his new wife. She had a child's loyalty and she resented her father's remarrying. Actually, Helen is a good woman—and she's been a good mother to Val. But as you've probably learned, Val can be very stubborn. So as soon as she was old enough, she left home. Both her dad and Helen were delighted when she let them know she was going to work for you. They wrote me a long letter telling me all about it as soon as they heard. I'll bet if she spent some time with her father now, she'd feel differently about the whole situation. Think you could help me persuade her to go?"

"I don't know. I'll do my best. I'm not too good at influencing people, I'm afraid."

Mark stopped, took me by the shoulders and turned me toward him. "Cris, are you really happy? Sometimes I get the feeling you can't wait for us to leave."

"Oh, Mark, don't say that! I hope you can stay all summer. And of course I'm happy. I just get tired, sometimes, when we hike too long. I'm sorry. I guess I do look a bit down when I get fatigued."

He did not release his hold. "I don't know why you're lying to me, Cris, but I know you too well. When you were a teenager you were sleek like a Siamese cat. Now you're more mature—but you still have that smoothness. I could tell then when you were truly happy. Your eyes had a depth that was kind of dark blue. When you pretended to be, the blue was shallow—sort of icy. That's how your eyes look to me now. Please, Crystal, I'm an old friend. You can tell me what's wrong."

I held myself still until I could control my voice. "Oh, Mark, please. You're an old friend, that's true. But we've forgotten a lot about each other in the years we've been apart. Are you so sure you can remember that much about my eyes?" I tried to be lighthearted, but I knew I sounded flippant, as if I didn't care about his feelings.

Diego seemed to sense trouble brewing. He broke between us and took our hands. "Hey! We're letting Pat and Val get ahead. Come on!" We ran together down the hill to where Valerie and Patrick were already romping in the cove.

An hour later, when we had tired of the water, we lay on the sand watching little Mimi, who had come down to join us. Suddenly Diego sat up.

"Crystal?" I nodded. "Remember what Dr. Reyes said about algae in the caves around Soledad?"

"Yes. They're not far from here. I expect they're the ones Lorenzo was exploring when we met."

"I was wondering . . . do you think Lorenzo would object to my borrowing some of his diving equipment? I could take a look for myself. If there really are rare types of algae . . . . I can't imagine the caves are too deep. A face mask might be enough."

Valerie began to laugh. "Don't be too sure, Diego! I went looking for coral one day, when Crystal was in Palma with Lorenzo. I'm a good underwater swimmer, and I never did reach bottom. I don't intend to try again—at least not without a wet suit for protection. When I surfaced, Miguel was on the yacht, sorting out some cables, and he warned me that there were eels and octopuses near the bottom. He said the eels were the dangerous kind."

Patrick sat up suddenly. "I had a similar experience—last year, before . . . ." He stopped for a moment and then continued. "I was swimming around at the bottom, near here, and I saw a giant grouper near the entrance to the cove. He was a beautiful specimen!" He turned to Valerie. "Groupers like rocky bottom land, and they're very territorial. Well, whenever I got close to this one, he'd just head for the cove. I couldn't follow him to the bottom; it's too deep. So I told Lorenzo about it."

"Oh, yes, I remember," I broke in. "He offered to lend you anything you needed. I was surprised. He doesn't like me to dive deep at all."

"Well, I can see why. Every time I tried to take him up on his offer, something went wrong. A mask strap broke, a zipper wouldn't zip, a tank valve malfunctioned. Once a tank was out of air when Miguel thought it was full. I was rather surprised. I thought Lorenzo took better care of his diving equipment—of everything he owns, for that matter." He paused for a moment, thinking. "Then . . . then things got too mixed up. I didn't have the time. But I really tried. I didn't want Lorenzo to think I was afraid."

"I guess you never heard. After . . . you left for England, Lorenzo bought all new equipment, and I heard him lecturing Miguel on proper maintenance. He must have had trouble with the old things, too."

Mark smiled mysteriously. "Aha! So the secret is out. Lorenzo and Miguel are the only two who have been to the bottom of the cove. I wonder what they found there? Pirates' treasure, maybe? Or just a few frightened eels."

I laughed. "No treasure—unfortunately. When I first came to Majorca, the coast guard was dredging the cove in search of a wrecked ship. They couldn't find anything. They were hunting around there on the same day I met Lorenzo—but he was closer to the cliffs, and when he surfaced he picked some flowers and put them in one of the bottles he'd brought up from the bottom."

I turned away, afraid Mark might see that my eyes were silver blue again. I didn't want him to read in them the pain and confusion for the empty ache that was my marriage. My memories of Lorenzo's courtship were like dried wild flowers, while love for Mark now bloomed in my heart. But he must never know. Not as long as Lorenzo was my husband. . . .

WORD CAME THE NEXT DAY from Palma. Lorenzo had departed for a visit to Lisbon that would last over a month. Diego received the news with obvious disappointment. Then he began to smile once more. "So, I'll wait. I think I'll take off for Sicily. There are some well-known grottoes there, too."

We could not dissuade him, and so the following day we watched him depart. Then, as luck would have it, Lorenzo returned unexpected a week later, laden with gifts for us all. Mimi, as usual, was more pleased with the handkerchief Miguel brought her than the fancy doll Lorenzo had purchased. Lorenzo seemed unable to relate to a child, even when he tried. He possessed very little family feeling and was generally content to be Mimi's "uncle," though I had hoped they would grow close.

I decided to try once more to find out why he was so indifferent to children. When Mimi left with Mark to join Patrick and Valerie at the beach, I took his arm. "What was your father like, Lorenzo? You've never told me."

His expression grew cold. "That's because I don't remember much about him, except that he was old—and stingy! He was a bad-tempered man who loved to hunt. He collected guns. I suppose he was born too late. He belonged back in the Middle Ages!"

"And your mother?"

"Poor mother. I didn't know her very well. She died when I was a child—and the infant she bore died, too. But I remember her as sad faced and beautiful." He shrugged, as if to brush the memory away. "Let's let the dead rest in peace. I don't want to talk about it anymore."

I nodded and led the way to the cove. I had learned nothing more than I already knew. And I felt that my questions only led him to believe I was spying on him.

I was, of course—but he was watching me, too. I sensed it more than ever before, for when Lorenzo himself was not at Soledad, Miguel was usually around, puttering on the yacht. I had hoped to use the yacht for some trips with my friends, but that was impossible—unless I wanted Miguel along.

This time, before Lorenzo returned to Palma, he made a point of convincing Mark that he should visit the grottoes for which Majorca is famous. He insisted that all four of us go—and as usual when he wanted to be, he was very convincing.

Mark suggested he come, too, since he seemed so

well acquainted with the grottoes, but Lorenzo refused. "I really can't take the time. I have a great deal
of work to do and I'm expecting an important client
tomorrow in Palma." He grinned boyishly. "Besides,
to be quite honest, I've seen the grottoes so often that
I know them like the palm of my hand—and they
rather bore me. I hope you'll understand."

"Maybe I ought to go with you," I offered, "to make
your client welcome."

"Oh, no, my dear! He's important—but he's not
a social guest. Purely business." He smiled at Mark.
"So it's settled. You can take the sailboat."

I agreed then, and we set about making plans. Lorenzo decided to wait at Soledad until we were on
our way, in case we needed help in getting started.
I wondered if he only wanted to be sure Patrick went
along. Because in spite of Patrick's promise to me that
he would delay any investigation until Mark was gone,
my brother was growing restless.

I sympathized with him—and I knew Valerie shared
his eagerness to begin the search for the Picasso. But
I would not allow him to do anything that would
make Mark think my life at Soledad was anything but
ideal. I dared not accept the possibility that Mark still
loved me, and I did not want to invite his pity.

The Arta Grotto was our first stop. We clambered
down the chiseled steps on the side of the mountain
to the ancient, vast cave with its incredible architecture dating back millions of years. The guide rambled
on, and I could see that Mark was fascinated. He
leaned close. "It's sensational! I'll have to bring Diego
back here. Lorenzo was right when he insisted we
see it."

I had almost forgotten Lorenzo. Now he stood between me and the momentary pleasure of an outing.
His eagerness to have me away from Soledad preyed
on me. "Do you mind? I'm getting chilly. I'll wait up
on the cliff."

Mark insisted on accompanying me, and despite my protests he led the way up the steps to a stone bench. He hovered over me, obviously worried. "Now that you've mentioned your malaise, Cris, I want to know. Val said she met you at a hospital in Paris. Were you in for something serious?" He paused. "I know it was a clinic that specializes in treating nervous breakdowns. Were your problems really so unmanageable?"

"Oh, no!" I forced myself to speak lightly. "I just had more trouble than I expected in getting over Alan's death—Mimi's father. He was killed in a terrorist attack on a passenger he was flying somewhere. It was so unnecessary . . . so meaningless."

Mark was silent. He glanced down the steps. Patrick and Valerie were approaching, and they both looked upset. "Ah—love's first fight! I hope it isn't serious. I really like the idea of those two getting married. First love is so precious. Irreplaceable."

"Maybe." I understood him too well. "But isn't the most important love the last one? It's the one that fills most of one's life."

"But how do you know it's the last? No, I think you're wrong. Only the first is unique—special." He rose as if afraid to continue the conversation. Then suddenly he bent down. "Cris, you're not happy—I can see that! And I could make you happy; I know I could. . . ."

I felt my emotions swell in response to him. I wanted to fling myself into his arms, tell him how much he meant to me. But it was impossible, and foolish. I refused to meet his pleading eyes. "Mark, please, you forget. I'm married!"

By the time Patrick and Valerie joined us we had all succeeded in concealing our individual perturbations. But the atmosphere had changed. I knew what had upset Valerie. Patrick had told her they could not marry until he cleared his name. And I was upset because I knew now that even if Mark and I never mentioned the subject again, I would not forget that he still loved me—and that I loved him.

In spite of our depressed spirits we visited every grotto on Lorenzo's list. There were times when we were able to recover our enthusiasm, but the general mood was still low as we turned at last toward home. Valerie and I sat together on the deck of the boat, soaking in the sun, and she finally unburdened herself. "Oh, Crystal, it's such a waste! I could help him! Why won't he see it my way?"

"Because you mean so much to him. Val, have you ever considered that your father might have some ideas to help you? From what Mark says, he's a very wise man. He might even be able to convince Patrick to see things your way." I thought for a moment. Mark had said something about Val's father and stepmother taking a trip to Europe—to stay in Monaco. "Isn't he going to be in Europe this summer?"

"Yes . . . but I hadn't intended to visit them."

"Oh, but you must! It would be terrible to have them come so close and not see them. Maybe Patrick could go with you."

I mentioned the idea to Lorenzo when we joined him for dinner in Palma, and he seemed delighted. "Of course!" he told Valerie. "You've done so well with Mimi, you deserve a vacation." He smiled his most winning smile. "I might even ask a favor of you. I have a package of precious stones that have to be delivered to a customer in Nice. Perhaps you wouldn't mind dropping it off for me, on your way."

Valerie agreed quickly. She seemed almost relieved at the opportunity to get away for a few days. On the drive back to Soledad she spoke with enthusiasm about her planned visit to her father. Both Mark and I were pleased. At least one problem—Valerie's rift with her father—promised to be solved.

When we reached Soledad I called Eulalia. Lorenzo

had seemed so pleased with himself—as if he had put something over on us all. I had to find out what had happened in our absence. "Eulalia? Did anyone come here while we were gone?"

"Oh, no, *señora*. No one was here." She paused. "Oh! Except the coast guard." She glanced at Incarnation, who was standing to one side, waiting for me to speak to her. "Felipe said he was here to inspect the entire west coast of the island, but I think he really came to see how his favorite girl was." Incarnation blushed. "He arrived before the *señor* and Miguel left for Palma, and Miguel insisted they search the boats in the cove. But nothing important happened." She smiled as she glanced again toward Incarnation. "And no one important arrived."

I dismissed the servants and returned to my room. Yet I couldn't rid myself of the feeling that something lay behind Lorenzo's insistence that I join Mark on his excursions. Was he hoping to catch me in an indiscretion? And why was he so friendly to Patrick?

I thought I knew the answer to that question. I was certain that he hoped to convince Patrick to let things be. Then I had a terrible thought. What if he was only trying to keep both of us placated until Mark and Diego had left? And now Valerie would be out of the way, too! When they were all gone, what plans did he have to end the search that Patrick—and I—were determined to pursue?

Chapter 15

A telegram arrived the next day, addressed to Mark. He read it in silence, then smiled. "Well! It seems my friend is at last growing tired of wandering. He's coming back to pick me up and we'll make one final trip to Italy. Then back home . . . at last."

He seemed pleased at the thought of leaving, but I did not share his joy. I knew he wanted to go—now—because I had made it clear that I was not willing to leave Lorenzo. Yet I knew I would miss him terribly. I kept my voice carefully under control. "When will you be leaving for Italy?"

"I expect in about three days. Diego plans to arrive here tomorrow."

Mimi appeared in the doorway—followed by Valerie. The time they reserved for classes was just ending. "Uncle Mark!" She bounced into the room and climbed onto his lap. "You said you had a present for me?"

"Oh, yes." He pulled a small box from his pocket. "I found this in my suitcase this morning. I'd forgotten all about it." He opened the box and took out two small figurines. "The children in Mexico love to play with them. The black one is the devil. His name is—"

"Zozobra!" Mimi was jumping up and down excitedly. "I know them both! The other is the good fairy, Schams. Am I right, Uncle Mark?"

"Yes, you are." He looked at me in surprise. "Where did she learn about these two? You haven't been to Mexico, have you?"

I shook my head. "I don't know. Mimi? Who told you about Zozobra and Schams?"

"Miguel!" She was quite proud to have a special secret. "He's got all sorts of little blue drawings on his chest—and some on his arms. He even has one of the feathered serpent. That one's sort of magic, because you can't really see the serpent—or the feathers. You know what it looks like, don't you, Uncle Mark?"

"Yes, I do. Quetzalcoatl. A legendary Mexican creature." He put her down and rose. "Run along and play now. And don't lose Schams."

"I won't. Thank you, Uncle Mark!" Mimi was gone, with Valerie close behind.

Mark's smile vanished. "Now I know where I saw your Miguel. He must have been a Mexican bullfighter at some time. I remember him now. He was quite good. Strong—and agile." He grew sober. "Crystal, we might not be coming back to Soledad. We might head straight for Gibraltar." He took my hands in his. "Are you sure . . . ?"

"Please, Mark, don't . . . spoil things."

He nodded. "Just one question. When we were at the Arta Grotto, I recalled another, smaller one—not really a grotto, of course, but a cave that we called the cave of the sea gulls. Remember it?"

I remembered it only too well. I turned away, to hide my face from his questioning gaze. "No, Mark, I don't remember it at all. We had all sorts of odd names for places when we were children."

I kept my face averted until I heard him leave. Then slowly I wiped the tears from my eyes.

THE FOLLOWING DAY Valerie and Patrick left for Monaco. Diego arrived that afternoon, and instead of disembarking he insisted that Mark join him immediately. There was some sort of festival in southern Italy that he wanted to observe before starting home, and they'd have to hurry to get there before it ended.

Lorenzo was present to see Diego and Mark off, and once more he took advantage of Diego's good nature to send a large art piece—a valuable vase—to Palermo, in Sicily. I was distraught at Mark's sudden departure, and annoyed that even at the last moment Lorenzo should think only of his own convenience. But Diego had no objections to making the stop, and the pair departed that afternoon. I stood on the shore holding Mimi's hand and wishing I dared to cry. Lorenzo was the first to turn from the sea and start back toward the house.

I let Mimi run ahead. I had a great need to be alone, to immerse myself in memories I had too long put aside. So many years had passed—and so much had happened. But Mark's visit had brought it all back. The salt smell of fish and damp sweaters. The howling of the wind as it blew off the ocean. The brisk mornings when we walked along the beach holding hands to keep warm. The realization of first love. The cave of the sea gulls. . . .

I longed for the release of tears but knew that once the flood came I'd be unable to stop it. I had been happy . . . once. Why had I forgotten? And now, when it was too late—why did I remember?

Soledad was quiet for the next while. In the excitement of the visits and departures I had forgotten my fear of being alone. Now it came back; I felt nervous, unsettled. But I had no cause for fright, for the days passed peacefully. We were not expecting guests until the middle of August. Lorenzo was in Palma much of the time, and when he did visit Soledad he seemed to sense my edgy mood and avoided confrontations.

I received a letter from Mark, written a few days after his departure. In it he reported that the vase had been safely delivered to the buyer's home though it had almost broken in a squall. As for the festival, it was delightful. The girls were beautiful, the music lilting—and the days sunny and warm. He and Diego had now decided to stay a bit longer in Italy. They were unsure yet whether they would stop at Soledad before starting home.

Mimi was disappointed. "Uncle Mark promised to bring me a bracelet. He can't forget!"

"Please, dear." I was comforting myself as well as my daughter. "He can't do everything he wanted to do. Remember, he's an important man back in Mexico—he can't stay away forever." I forced a smile. "Besides, he doesn't say for certain that he won't stop here again."

I didn't believe he'd return, despite my assurance to Mimi. What could he find here but more frustration? And I would be thrown again into a turmoil. I wanted peace, and I knew I could achieve at least an empty kind of peace only when I knew Mark was gone for good.

I was relieved when a letter arrived from Valerie. She and Patrick were enjoying their visit with her father and stepmother. To her surprise, Helen seemed quite different. Gentle, and very sympathetic; not at all the ogre she had appeared to be when Valerie was younger. I chuckled as I read her letter. Valerie had grown up, and she now recognized the good in her stepmother to which her childish hostility had previously blinded her.

Dr. Reyes dropped by that afternoon. He frowned when he saw my pallor. "You've been neglecting

yourself. You need exercise. It was wonderful when
your old friend was here. How is he, by the way?
And how's Valerie doing with her parents?"

I showed him Valerie's letter. But I found it difficult
to speak of Mark. Could I admit that I saw him at
every turn in the garden? That I still felt his presence
when I stepped onto the terrace to watch the sunset?
That I heard his laughter in the sound of the waves?

Dr. Reyes lifted my arm and felt my pulse. "You
need a change, my dear. Why don't you go to Minorca? You know how much Catalina enjoys your
visits."

I shook my head. "Later, please. I'm really very
busy now. Lorenzo has so many customers . . . ." I
did not finish my sentence, hoping Dr. Reyes would
accept the excuse that I was busy helping my husband.

A week later I decided to drive into Pollensa to
shop. I left Mimi with her nurse, though she begged
me to let her come along. I had to be alone. I was
growing frantic for a chance to let my emotions out.

I headed for the bazaar, hoping to find a bracelet
that would serve as a substitute for the one Mark
would not be bringing to Mimi. And it was there, in
a small jewelry shop, that I came upon him. "Mark!"

He looked up, startled, like a boy caught at some
mischief. "Crystal! What are you doing here?"

"I shop here! What are you doing here? I thought
you were still in Italy."

"Are you alone?" When I nodded, he continued,
"Then come with me. I'll explain everything."

He took me by the arm and led me from the shop.
We went into a small café and sat in a secluded booth.
I noticed that the carving on a nearby wine cask was
garnished with a string of garlic and pimento. It seemed
out of place, somehow. Little nothings with which
I distracted myself to avoid looking at Mark.

When he did not immediately begin, I spoke. "Where's Diego?"

"In Alcudia, helping friends with their boat. He'll be back tomorrow. The *Cris* is anchored in Puerto. We arrived last night."

"You were going to leave without seeing us again? Mimi has been looking for you every day! Weren't you even going to call?"

He started to reach for my hand, then drew his own hand back. "Please, Crystal, you must understand. I realized I'd gone a bit too far—before we left. I had no right to . . . ." He paused. "How is your hu—Lorenzo?"

"Fine." There was a tremor in my voice. "He went to Barcelona this morning. I expect him back tomorrow. Valerie and Patrick are still in Monaco, but I suppose you know that." My voice broke. "I was just getting ready to invite myself to Dr. Reyes's house for lunch. I didn't want to be alone, after all."

"Really? Then have lunch with me. Here, in Pollensa? Manacor? Inca?" You name the place! He was playing the gallant, and I responded to his high spirits. "Does madam wish lunch in a palace—or in a modest inn? Or better yet, how about a sandwich aboard the *Cris*?"

I felt safe again. He would not allow us to slip back into seriousness. "Anyplace. Just let me call Eulalia so she won't wait lunch for me."

By the time I returned from making the call, I felt at ease again. We had put the past behind us. And we had one day we could spend as we wished. I wanted to savor every minute of it, for it would be the last we shared.

We bought sandwiches and a bottle of wine at a stand and then drove in my car to the port. I grabbed my swimsuit from the trunk, and we boarded the *Cris* amid much laughter. I stood on deck like a captain issuing orders. "Head west! Full speed!" Mark set sail without further questions.

It took an hour for us to reach my favorite spot. I had named it The Shell, because its shape reminded me of a Coquille St.-Jacques. I had visited the place many times before, with Mimi, but otherwise it was my secret. A totally primitive beach, where the only footsteps I saw were my own.

We anchored offshore and took the dinghy to the island. "Do you come here often?" Mark asked as he nosed the dinghy onto the sand.

"No. Only when I feel depressed—or want some peace."

"You're not depressed now, are you?" He seemed upset. "I hoped we could keep things . . . on a better plane."

"Oh, no. I'm fine now. Let's fish!"

When we caught fish we roasted and ate them instead of the sandwiches. Then we raced about like children at play, and at last, exhausted, lay down to sun ourselves and sleep.

I woke feeling warm—and very happy. Mark was sitting beside me, studying my features. "Do you really want me to drop back at Soledad, Crystal? I must confess I'd like to see the place again—and say a decent goodbye to Mimi. I don't like to disappoint a child."

"Yes. Please stay a few days before you head home. I think it will be all right now that we've—" I hesitated only a moment. "—straightened things out between us."

"Good!" He pointed up the cliff. "Look! A cave! Have you ever climbed to it?"

I shook my head. "I haven't dared to go up alone. But it's always reminded me of the cave of the gulls."

Without answering, Mark led the way up the rocks. The view was beautiful, and we sat together quietly gazing out at the sea. At last he spoke. "You did remember, didn't you? Why did you tell me you didn't?"

"I guess I was afraid. But I'm sure we both understand now that we can't go back to the past."

He nodded. We sat in silence, remembering. It had been a warm day, and we had climbed together to see the cave. On the way I had skinned my shoulder, and Mark bent to kiss it. We were both aware—so terribly aware—of each other. Aware . . . and uneasy.

His lips had moved to my neck, and then to my lips. It was the moment of discovery. The awakening of love for us both. I clung to him with all my strength, wanting him to stay near me, in my arms, forever.

Then Mary had called to us, and the magic spell was broken. The next day Mark had returned to medical school—and a week later I was in Europe, with my parents.

"Why didn't you write, Mark?"

"I wanted to, but I was afraid I'd sound sentimental. It had happened so suddenly—and it ended so quickly—I wasn't sure it had meant the same to you as it did to me. And then I was busy, too, and you seemed so distant. I'd always been aware that your folks were rich and mine were poor. Why didn't you write to me?"

"I suppose I was too shy," I confessed. "It had meant so much to me—and I thought if it meant anything at all to you, you'd let me know. When I never heard from you, I was hurt." I sighed. "Oh, Mark. We were so foolish!"

I don't know who moved first, but suddenly we were in each other's arms, clinging together as we had that day so long ago. He kissed me and then he pushed me away. "Oh, Crystal, I've been going crazy! I wanted to forget—to put you behind me. But I can't. I was in torture at Soledad, knowing you belonged to someone else. When I saw you at Doña Catalina's in Minorca I knew why I've never been able to take another woman seriously."

His words tore at my heart. "You don't want to come to Soledad, do you?" I asked him softly.

"Not really. It still hurts. Oh, don't get me wrong; I'm not contemplating stealing you away at the last moment. But I've been tempted. Just remember, if you ever need me I'll come back. I know now I can never care for any other woman as I care for you."

I did not move. "Mark . . . ." My heart ached, but I dared not let him know. "I think it will be better if you do come to Soledad—at least for a short farewell. People in Pollensa have seen us together, and people talk. I'll invite Dr. Reyes, too, so things will be comfortable."

He nodded. "If that's what you wish. Just remember, I still have a part of you." He gestured toward the bow of the *Cris*.

"If you ever change the name, I'll know—" He didn't allow me to continue. Once more he pressed his lips to mine. I didn't pull away. Two passionate kisses—and so many years between. How could they be so similar, so powerful, when there had been an eternity between them?

Our embrace seemed to last forever—too short a time. Finally I pulled away. I knew my resolve was weakening. "Please, Mark, let's leave now."

As we approached the shore, Mark spoke. "Are you sure you want us to come for dinner?"

"Yes, please. People won't wonder, if you're still Lorenzo's friend as well as mine. Look!" I pointed to the ridge. "The white flag is flying. Lorenzo is back already."

Chapter 16

Lorenzo was in a foul mood, and he wouldn't tell me why. However, he had brought me a camera—not, certainly, the first he had purchased. We had many at Soledad, and though each saw a great deal of use in the first days after its purchase, we usually forgot about them in the weeks that followed.

I told him "the Mexicans" were coming for a farewell visit, and he seemed pleased. "At least we'll have some variety in our pictures. And I'm sure you'll be glad to have a few permanent souvenirs of your friends' visit. Tell me, why didn't you marry Mark Lefevre? He still seems very fond of you."

I felt a momentary panic. Had someone said something to him about us? Had we been seen in the cove? Then the panic passed. There was nothing Lorenzo could do to me that mattered. "Because, my dear husband, it was written somewhere that I was to be Lorenzo Santos's wife!"

He looked surprised—maybe even troubled. I felt sure his eyes showed a momentary regret. For what, I wondered. For what had been done—or attempted? Or for what he planned in the future? I decided not to press the question. I would find out soon enough.

"I also invited Don Cristobal Reyes." I felt cool—collected. On top of everything. "How is Dolores? How was the weather in Palma?"

His voice was steady. "Dolores is fine, but exhausted. We've been working very hard and there's a heat wave in Palma. Don't you feel the humidity here, too? We don't usually get storms this time of year, but I feel one on the way."

"Yes, I've felt it. I thought it might break last night, but nothing happened. I wish it would start soon. Then we'd be through with all this moisture . . . and the heat!"

The weather did not change during the next twenty-four hours. Mark and Diego arrived for dinner, accompanied by Dr. Reyes. We stood for a while watching the darkening sky. Then Diego spoke. "Odd! I can't hear any insects. Isn't that unusual this early in the evening?"

I listened, but I could hear no natural sounds. It was eerie—uncomfortable. "Let's go in and eat." I spoke nervously. "Maybe everything will be back to normal later."

Conversation was slow, as if we were all waiting for some unknown arrival. Then suddenly a flash of lightning illumined the sky. Diego looked up. "How strange! Lightning without thunder. The storm must be very far away."

"It probably will reach Majorca in about an hour," Don Cristobal answered. "Sometimes these summer storms are worth watching. Marvelous fireworks . . . very beautiful."

"Is Mimi afraid of lightning?" Mark seemed disappointed still that I had insisted the child go to bed at her usual time.

"Oh, no. Mimi isn't afraid of anything! Listen—you can hear her laughing with her nurse."

Lorenzo frowned. "All I can hear is Felipe, chattering with Incarnation. Isn't he supposed to be on duty?"

"I suppose not. I saw him in the kitchen just before we sat down to dinner. I'm sure he's glad to be out of the storm. The seas can get very rough. But I think he said something about being on a special mission that was to start around midnight. Poor boy! He'll hit the storm at its peak." I paused. "I wonder what's so important it would force the coast guard out to sea at a time like this?"

"I understand from my friends in Alcudia that some plutonium is missing from the atomic research laboratory. Maybe that's what they're searching for," Diego suggested.

"Yes, yes, of course." Lorenzo seemed almost relieved. "Everyone's been talking about it in Palma, too. There's so much traffic in the port at Palma, it's too much to ask the coast guard to keep track of it all."

"Felipe didn't mention plutonium. But he did do a lot of talking—I suppose to impress Incarnation. Let's see . . . he was telling about a new vessel the guard saw, a new minisub that's supposed to be smuggling an enormous cargo of drugs. They're going to follow it ashore and raid the place where it drops the cargo. Sounds exciting, doesn't it?"

Lorenzo muttered a curse under his breath. His hand had slipped as he poured my wine, and now the carafe lay shattered at his feet. He knelt to pick up the largest pieces. "Excuse me. I'll get another from the cellar." He turned from the table.

"Don't bother, Lorenzo, please!" Don Cristobal held out a hand in protest. "We can finish our dinner with one of the domestic wines you have on the table."

But Lorenzo was adamant. He hurried to the cellar. I sat for a moment, waiting for his return. Then, aware of the awkwardness of the delay, I rose. "Why don't we all go out on the terrace and wait for him? I'd like to get a better look at the storm as it approaches."

We stood together admiring the contrast of light and dark in the western sky. "Fantastic!" Diego exclaimed, pointing toward the horizon.

"It's a true electrical storm. Early for the year." Don Cristobal beamed with pleasure. "They always fascinate me. Your aunt used to watch them from the tower."

"What a marvelous idea!" I felt elated. "Let's finish dinner and climb the tower ourselves. If we hurry, we can get there before the rain starts."

Lorenzo stepped onto the terrace. "Here's the wine. I wonder if you will forgive me . . . I just bought a new camera, and I want to try to get some shots of the storm as it approaches. The light is fantastic!"

Don Cristobal stood with his hand on the terrace railing. "We have decided we want to climb to the tower and watch the storm," he told Lorenzo. "Why don't you come with us? I'm sure you can get great pictures from there."

"Yes, why don't we have dessert later," I suggested, "after we've had our fun with the storm. Lorenzo, will you come with us?"

He hesitated, and in that instant Miguel appeared at the door to the dining room. "Señor Santos, everything is in readiness. I am waiting to take you, as soon as you are prepared to depart."

Lorenzo nodded. "Crystal, I hope you and your friends will forgive me. I've already made arrangements with Miguel to take the yacht out so I can get photographs of the storm as it hits the island. They should be marvelous."

I stared at him in horror. Go to sea, in the face of such a storm? No one in his right mind would do a thing like that! Before I could reply, Don Cristobal stepped toward Lorenzo. "My dear man, you can't mean to be so foolish. To go out in this kind of a storm is sheer folly!"

Lorenzo began to laugh. "Please, doctor! Miguel is a strong man, capable of holding a wheel in the worst storm. And besides, I'm not the kind to take great risks. Yet a bit of controlled excitement lends spice to living!"

He turned to the door. "Come along, Miguel. We'll be safer when we get beyond the entrance to the cove." He bowed to the doctor. "Don Cristobal, I'll send you a print of the film when I'm finished. It should be exceptionally spectacular."

He was gone before any of us could object. I felt shocked. On previous occasions he had shown some recklessness, but never anything as unusual as this urge to fight the forces of nature.

Diego shrugged. "Spoken like a true compulsive gambler. The day comes when it isn't enough to risk capital. Then one must take the greatest gamble of all—the gamble with one's own life."

I shuddered. Mark touched my shoulder. "I'm sure he'll be all right. Why don't we go up to the tower right away. We can watch him—as well as the storm."

Mark seemed not to have lost his childhood ability to see in the dark. He led the way up the hill, with Diego behind him. I followed, and Dr. Reyes, who was accustomed to walking at night, took up the rear. We almost collided with a herd of sheep hurrying to shelter, and the odor of their damp fur reminded me again of the farms that bordered the coast of Connecticut. I would never forget those days, I knew that. I could only hope that all of my memories would someday return with a little less pain.

Mark paused at the foot of the tower and let Don Cristobal and Diego go ahead. He turned back and gestured toward the house. "It looks so strange, doesn't it? Crystal, is it only my imagination that Soledad seems oppressed with impending tragedy? And terribly lonely?"

I shuddered. The tragedy I saw ahead was his departure. The strangeness—the solitude—was in our hearts. He would be fortunate to get free of this place—and of me. Then I forced myself to speak brightly. "Yes, I see what you mean. But I'm afraid the island is always like this before a storm. It all clears up when the rain begins."

The view from the tower was magnificent. The sky was a continuous series of lightning bolts. Angry clouds fought each other for dominance in the western horizon. The water was a phosphorescent green, with whitecaps breaking up the solid color. And behind us the purple mountains glowered as if daring the storm to attack.

Diego threw out his arms in a grand gesture. "This, my friends, is nature at her most impressive. What power!"

"Listen!" Mark held up one hand. "You can hear the thunder, at last."

"We can see it! That lightning is striking somewhere!" Don Cristobal peered down toward the cove. "Let's pray that Lorenzo has run out of film and is back in the harbor."

As he spoke, lightning flashed across the sky. We could see clearly the coast, the rough water, Lorenzo's yacht, still moving away from the shore. I gasped. "Oh, look!"

"He's insane!" Mark was at my side. "No one can take pictures in that rough a sea. His camera will be bouncing all over the place."

"Why doesn't he come in?" I leaned forward.

Dr. Reyes took my arm. "Get hold of yourself, my dear. You can't signal to him from here. He'll do what he wants. Isn't that what he's always done? You couldn't have stopped him from going out tonight, you know that." He, too, leaned forward. "I can't understand him. He's still heading out—right into the worst of the storm!''

Mark pointed somewhat to the left of the yacht. "Wait! It looks as if the coast guard is going to his rescue. He'll be fine.''

But Lorenzo's boat did not turn toward the coast-guard cutter. It seemed, instead, to be running away. I called out, but of course Lorenzo could not hear me. And then, as we watched helplessly, the space between the two boats widened. There was no denying what was happening. Lorenzo knew the guard was near—and he was running away!

Diego saw the big wave first. He shouted, and we all gazed horrified in the direction he pointed. It moved steadily forward . . . and then enveloped the yacht. The little coast-guard cutter bounced helplessly on the crest, but it retained its buoyancy. When the wave had passed, Lorenzo's yacht was gone, swallowed by the sea.

Chapter 17

I don't know how I reached the house, or who helped me into my bed. I was in shock. I woke once to hear voices, but I was too upset to move, and so I dropped back into a restless sleep. In the morning I learned the worst.

Dr. Reyes had remained beside me throughout the night. He had given me a sleeping pill, though I had fought it at first. When he saw my eyes open he hurried to the bed. "Crystal, my dear, I fear the worst has happened. The yacht is lost . . . and Lorenzo is dead."

He held my hand and squeezed it in sympathy. "Miguel is still alive. The coast guard pulled him out of the water." He held up his hand to signal that he was not yet through speaking. "They will be here shortly. I think it best if you are up when they arrive."

Mark, Diego and Don Cristobal stood beside me when the coast guard arrived. The officer in charge glanced at the men. "Madam, I think you might wish to hear me without witnesses."

"No, I prefer that my friends be present. Please continue."

"Madam, we have a most difficult duty to perform.

I have here a search warrant. We are under orders to go through all of Soledad."

"Search warrant? What for?"

"I regret it most sincerely," he apologized. "We have reason to believe there may be some twenty-five kilos of heroin on the property. The chauffeur has made a full confession, but he merely confirmed what our investigation had already led us to suspect. You understand, madam, we know you are not aware of any of this matter, and we will do all we can to minimize your inconvenience."

I stepped back. "Please, go ahead with your search. I am sure you will find nothing."

My words seemed prophetic. It was not until the next day, when they returned with new warrants, that the entire matter came out. Lorenzo was, in truth, the head of a large narcotics ring. Dolores and Miguel were his immediate accomplices, but Peraldez and many of his other "regular" customers were in on the conspiracy.

Lorenzo had a most clever scheme for moving his drugs. Every package he sent out with my friends held heroin, hidden in secret compartments. And even more shocking to me was the information that Valerie's car had been used to bring large supplies of the drug to Majorca from France. She and Patrick hurried back to be with me, and she was surprised when her car was confiscated by the authorities.

We understood now why Miguel had risked his life to keep Val's car from falling to the docks that day she had first arrived in Majorca. He wasn't worried about the vehicle. What he feared was that the drugs would be found, if he could not first unload them.

The shock was a great one, for I realized I had done my share of transporting drugs, as well. Every time I went to Paris, or to any of the cities along the coast of France, Spain or Italy, I had taken with me some package from Lorenzo to a "good client." We were the reason he had been so hard to catch.

The Picasso turned up at last in a secret closet at the gallery. It had been used for only one reason—to get Patrick away from Soledad when he began to show too much interest in deep-sea diving. We got permission to dive with the coast-guard investigators, and learned the true extent of Lorenzo's perfidy.

He had discovered that a small grotto, well above the waterline, was only accessible by diving under a reef near one end of the cove. It was there he hid the greatest part of his drug supply, wrapped in water-proof containers.

The Mercedes, too, was used in the transport of the drugs. And when Valerie saw the many compartments, her eyes widened. "I see it all now. The Mercedes must have been full of drugs that night when Miguel hit me. No wonder they didn't want the police brought in! My hospitalization was a small price to pay to keep their secret." She took my hand. "I can't regret that part of all this. If it had happened any differently, I'd never have met you—or Patrick."

The investigation continued for many days. Mark and Diego decided to delay their return to Mexico until everything was settled, and I found their presence most comforting.

Most of the conspirators were sent immediately to prison. Dolores, however, was put into a hospital for treatment as a drug addict. Finally her odd moods were explained. Yet I felt sorry for her. Lorenzo had led her to believe he wanted to marry her, maintaining the deception to keep her in his power. She was, after all, the main contact between him and his buyers.

I understood, also, what had precipitated the tragedy on the night of the storm. I had unwittingly alerted Lorenzo to the danger that lay in wait for the minisub. He had been forced to make an attempt to warn it away and had not dared to use ship-to-shore communication. He was sure the coast guard would monitor all wave bands. The idea of taking pictures had been the only ready solution he could find—and it had been a poor one.

When the commotion finally was over, Mark agreed to accompany me on a special pilgrimage to the Spanish mainland. Now, when it was too late to help him, I had to learn what I could about my unfortunate husband.

There was no village of Corpierro, the name Lorenzo had given as his birthplace. Yet we searched surrounding towns and finally located the birthplace of Miguel. And that led us to the truth of Lorenzo's sad life.

He and Miguel were both born in the village of Colpiedo, a small, almost deserted town high in the hills. I headed for the church and was lucky enough to find an elderly priest who, when I showed him Miguel's photograph, remembered his face.

"Ah, yes. Little Miguel Barreras. I christened him. He was a strange little boy—so devoted to his friend. . . ."

I pulled out a photograph of Lorenzo. "Is this his friend?"

"Yes! Lorenzo Santos. What a sad child! Poor boy! The illegitimate son of the last lord of Algeciras. His father refused to acknowledge him, though any fool could see the resemblance. His mother was broken by the shame. A real victim of circumstances—a laundrywoman in the château. Died when Lorenzo was only about eight. It was then the poor boy's father finally decided to send him off to school. He tried to pretend he was concerned for the child, but I knew he was too embarrassed by Lorenzo's close resemblance to him. I fear the lad was very bitter. He hated Colpiedo—and everything about it."

He looked again at the picture of Miguel. "I wonder,

did he ever become a toreador? The dreams children weave—sometimes they are very pathetic."

Mark spoke up. "I can assure you he did get to fight in the bullring. I watched him many times—in Mexico City."

The old man seemed pleased. "Well, I'm glad that one of them achieved his dream. Lorenzo, poor child, had more ambitious fantasies. He wanted to become a wealthy man . . . to have power . . . to control the lives of many people."

I looked up at Mark. "He reached his goal, too, padre. I think I understand now that, in a way, he died a happy man." I spoke again before he could question me further about Lorenzo. "Can you tell me where he grew up? You see, he was drowned recently. This is sort of a religious pilgrimage—to help him rest in peace."

When I stood in front of the dreary little hovel that was Lorenzo's birthplace, I knew only sorrow for the troubled, embittered man who had been my husband. He had sought and attained success—but it was never enough. I felt I could forgive him the grief he had caused me and others, for he had cut himself off from the potential pain of human emotions and could not see beyond his own lust for power. And now, I hoped, he was at rest. . . .

A few months afterward I agreed to Mark's continued requests that we follow Patrick and Valerie to the altar. Their wedding was a delightful, happy affair, with many of the island residents attending. Leaving the *Cris* at Soledad, Mark flew briefly to Mexico with Diego Sorlantes to clear up his hospital practice. Dr. Reyes, meanwhile, was thrilled at the prospect of taking on an energetic young partner to help out with his patients.

It was Mark who suggested we wait until Diego could return before setting our wedding date. I found it easy to accept the delay, for he remained with me at

Soledad, playing with Mimi as if she was his own daughter, and making every moment special. And last week a letter finally came from Diego, promising that he would be here this month to celebrate our wedding.

Later, Mark came up beside me as I stood gazing out to sea. "Darling, soon our wait will be over. Mimi will have a real family again . . . and maybe, in time, brothers and sisters. Things are starting over again, Crystal, and this time they're going to come out right— for us all."

A PASSPORT
TO ROMANCE...

A JOURNEY
INTO DANGER!

Join the thousands of readers
who have discovered the lure of

MYSTIQUE
BOOKS®

An exciting blend of
all you need to keep you reading
till the very last page!

Don't be left behind.

MYSTIQUE BOOKS®

MYSTIQUE BOOKS

Experience the warmth of love...
and the threat of danger!

MYSTIQUE BOOKS are a breathless blend of romance and suspense, passion and mystery. Let them take you on journeys to exotic lands—the sunny Caribbean, the enchantment of Paris, the sinister streets of Istanbul.

MYSTIQUE BOOKS

An unforgettable reading experience.
Now... many previously published titles are once again available.
Choose from this great selection!

Don't miss any of these thrilling novels of love and adventure!

Choose from this list of exciting
MYSTIQUE BOOKS